CAMBRIDGE STUDIES IN AMERICAN LITERATURE AND CULTURE

Wallace Stevens: The Poetics of Modernism

Cambridge Studies in American Literature and Culture

Editor:
Albert Gelpi, Stanford University

Advisory Board

Nina Baym, *University of Illinois, Champaign-Urbana*
Sacvan Bercovitch, *Harvard University*
Richard Bridgman, *University of California, Berkeley*
David Levin, *University of Virginia*
Joel Porte, *Harvard University*
Mike Weaver, *Oxford University*

Books in the Series

Contents

v

Preface

The essays included here address Wallace Stevens in distinctive voices, and one of the purposes of this collection is to present in concert six critics of twentieth-century poetry who have not previously published much, if anything, about Stevens – critics who are not, in any case, members of the Stevens critical establishment. His work has rightly commanded the attention of some of our ablest critics, particularly since the fifties, and the results have been extremely illuminating. But in the process something of a consensus approach has emerged, concentrated on explicating the strategies for fictionalizing the interaction of the imagination and reality into poems. The essays in this volume hope to contribute to a new phase of Stevens criticism from a number of intersecting and overlapping perspectives.

At the same time, these essays are less like a mere collection than they are like the chapters of a book because they are all engaged in a common venture: namely, specifying Stevens' place in the evolution of Modernist poetics in English. The Modernist period is framed and defined by the world wars. Modernism began to transform twentieth-century art, literature, and music in the years just before World War I, became the dominant aesthetic mode in the twenties, persisted through the challenge of Marxist criticism during the Depression, and gave way after World War II to a new generation of artists and writers that we now call, all too vaguely, Postmodernist. Nevertheless, that very epithet, for all its imprecision, reflects the continuing presence of Modernism as an informing influence and point of departure. Taken together, the essays in this book span the decades from the teens and twenties to the present and locate Stevens in the twentieth century literary scene all the way from his Modernist contemporaries like Ezra Pound, William Carlos Williams, and Marianne Moore to our own contemporaries like John Ashbery and Robert Duncan.

Each of the first group of essays, under the rubric "Stevens in Context," seeks to clarify Stevens' position by testing it against another set of terms or norms. My essay on the epistemology of Modernism juxtaposes Stevens and Williams as representatives of the Symboliste and Imagist traditions and argues that those two ongoing movements in twentieth-century poetry constitute a dialectic within Modernism about the nature of poetry itself. Gerald Bruns brings to bear on a number of the same issues the perspective of recent Postmodernist critical theories; he adopts a hermeneutical rather than an epistemological approach to Stevens, invoking Bakhtin to demonstrate the contemporaneity of Stevens' assumptions about the self-enclosure of the poet's act of language. Marjorie Perloff questions such antisocial aestheticism by examining the hermeticism of "Notes toward a Supreme Fiction," Stevens' most elaborate verse statement of his position, against the historical and political context of the war years in which it was composed and published. Closing out the first section are two views of Stevens' response to modern painting. Bonnie Costello anatomizes Stevens' frequent invocations of painting, particularly Impressionist and Postimpressionist painting, as an analogy for his kind of poetry, and delineates both the pertinence and the limits of that analogy. Charles Altieri resumes a number of these themes from a different perspective. Again taking up the epistemological issue, Altieri maintains that Stevens adopted the abstraction of modern art as a mode of signifying that was not limited or compromised by the disillusioning contradictions of history, and that such abstract passages sought to express transpersonal, shared values that enhanced the psychological and ethical life of the poet and his reader.

The last two essays present "Stevens as Context" for poets of later generations. Alan Golding follows up and to some extent qualifies my earlier discussion of Stevens and Williams by demonstrating that Louis Zukofsky, for all his Objectivist identification with Williams at midcentury, owed a profound and overlooked debt to Stevens as well. Michael Davidson returns to "Notes" as a touchstone to show how Stevens' poetic stance has been adopted by poets of the sixties and later, including not only Ashbery and Duncan but also Charles Olson, James Merrill, and Ed Dorn.

By speaking and responding to one another, extending and questioning one another, the essays in this book argue historically and speculatively for Stevens' centrality to American poetry throughout the century. They can be read separately, but they take on additional dimensions of referentiality and connection within the constellation of the book. It has been a pleasure to work with my colleagues on this shared venture. We have found both our points of agreement and our different perspectives clarifying, and we hope that others will find them so.

Albert Gelpi

Contributors

Charles Altieri is Professor of English at the University of Washington in Seattle. He has written *Enlarging the Temple: New Directions in Contemporary American Poetry; Act and Quality: A Theory of Literary Meaning;* and *Self and Sensibility in Contemporary American Poetry,* a volume in the Cambridge Studies in American Literature and Culture series.

Gerald L. Bruns is the William P. and Hazel B. White Professor of English at the University of Notre Dame. His critical works include *Words in the Void, Modern Poetry and the Idea of Language,* and *Inventions, Writing, Textuality and Understanding in Literary History.*

Bonnie Costello teaches at Boston University and is the author of *Marianne Moore: Imaginary Possessions,* which has won the Explicator Award. She has been in residence at the Bunting Institute at Radcliffe on a Rockefeller grant, working on *Elizabeth Bishop and the Tradition of the Beholder.*

Michael Davidson is a member of the Literature Department at the University of California, San Diego, and director of the Archive for New Poetry there. *The Mutabilities* gathered together earlier volumes of his poetry; his most recent volume is *The Prose of Fact.* He is writing the first book-length critical examination of its kind, *The San Francisco Poetry Renaissance,* for Cambridge Studies in American Literature and Culture.

Albert Gelpi is the William Robertson Coe Professor of American Literature at Stanford University. He is the author of *Emily Dickinson: The Mind of the Poet* and *The Tenth Muse: The Psyche of the American Poet,* and editor of the anthologies *The Poet in America 1650 to the Present* and, with Barbara Charlesworth Gelpi, *Adrienne Rich's Poetry.* A sequel to *The Tenth Muse* entitled *A Coherent Splendor: The American Poetic Renaissance 1910–1930* is forthcoming.

Alan Golding teaches twentieth-century poetry at the University of Mississippi. His articles and reviews have appeared in *Chicago Review, Language and Style, Arizona Quarterly, Poe Studies,* and in the University of Chicago Press collection *Carons.* An essay on Ed Dorn is in press, and he is writing a book on the history of the American poetry canon.

Marjorie Perloff is the Florence R. Scott Professor of English at the University of Southern California and author of *Rhyme and Meaning in the Poetry of Yeats, The Poetic Art of Robert Lowell, Frank O'Hara: Poet among Painters,* and *The Poetics of Indeterminacy: Rimbaud to Cage.* She is preparing a collection of her essays for publication in Cambridge Studies in American Literature and Culture under the title, *The Dance of the Intellect: Studies in the Poetry of the Pound Tradition,* and completing a book entitled *The Futurist Moment: Avant-Garde, Avant-Guerre, and the Language of Rupture.*

I

Stevens in Context

1

Stevens and Williams: The Epistemology of Modernism

ALBERT GELPI

1

It is difficult to be precise about the date and circumstances of the meeting between Wallace Stevens and William Carlos Williams, but it occurred late in the decade of the teens, when each was testing out his poetic voice and presence while struggling to establish a livelihood in another demanding, time-consuming profession: insurance law for Stevens, medicine for Williams. As poets, both had taken a course different from that of expatriates like Pound and Eliot, already internationally acclaimed by the avant-garde. Stevens and Williams would make their names more slowly in urban, industrial, corporate America, pursuing professional careers on opposite sides of the New York vortex: Stevens in Hartford, Connecticut, and Williams in Rutherford, New Jersey.

There was, then, good reason for them to regard each other with sympathy and respect from the start. The "Prologue" to *Kora in Hell,* dated September 1, 1918 – Williams' first polemical contribution to the ferment that was generating a Modernist poetics for the English-speaking world – cited a long letter from Stevens alongside missives from Pound and H.D. in London. Stevens' first volume, *Harmonium* (1923), included a 1918 poem entitled "Nuances of a Theme by Williams." They saw one another from time to time at gatherings of the New York group that published *Others* in the late teens. Stevens reported that a long-anticipated meeting with Williams in the summer of 1922 was "a blessing . . . though we were both as nervous as two belles in new dresses."[1] When the Objectivist Press, under the editorial guidance of Louis Zukovsky and George Oppen, offered to reissue Williams' poetry – out of print from small presses – Williams asked not Pound, as one might have expected in those Objectivist circles, but Stevens to supply the introduction to his *Collected Poems 1921–1931.*

3

And something of that comradely feeling endured to the end. When Williams seemed vulnerable or threatened, Stevens rallied to his side. Trying to coax Williams from one of his periodic depressions, Stevens congratulated him on an award from the National Institute of Arts and Letters in 1948: "You deserve everything that is coming your way."[2] After Williams' stroke in 1951, Stevens wrote: "You have worked hard all your life and now that you are at the top and need only time and the care of old age and leisure, I hope that what has happened will lead to some resolve (or to the necessity) to be more saving of what you have left."[3] After Williams had been prevented from becoming the consultant in poetry at the Library of Congress during the witch hunts of the fifties because of his leftist affiliations, Stevens' loyalty to Williams proved even stronger than his right-wing alarm at cries of communist conspiracy: "Williams is one of the few people in this country that really has an active and constant interest in writing."[4]

On his side, Williams considered Stevens "his most worthy American contender" and told him (with a Poundian combination of arrogance and condescension) that the two of them constituted "an elder group who are, in fact, in themselves, a critique and a *vade mecum* of an art that is slowly acquiring reality here in our God-forsaken territory."[5] Noting that his haste in writing the *Autobiography* against a publisher's deadline had made for regrettable omissions, Williams made it known through the preface that although Stevens was "scarcely mentioned" in the text, "he is constantly in my thoughts."[6] In fact, Williams' 1951 stroke precluded what would have been a major public event in modern poetry: the reunion of the two poets on stage at a convocation of Bard College that awarded Stevens an honorary degree, a sequel to Williams' honorary degree the previous year.[7]

Deeper than the biographical link between Williams and Stevens was the fact that they were engaged in parallel ventures of profound importance to literary Modernism: Among the major American poets of the High Modernist period they stood together as the two who most explicitly argued for, and premised their poetry upon, the primacy of the imagination. By the early twentieth century the character and efficacy of the imagination were, at the very least, much in doubt. Eighteenth-century Neoclassicism had taken the imagination as the ability to devise effective imagery. It was only one of various mechanically conceived faculties of the mind, to be coordinated and regulated by right reason and common sense. During the Romantic period, however, Coleridge redefined the imagination as the supreme cognitive faculty, a kind of mystical or metaphysical intuition – what the Neoclassicists had called imagination, Coleridge called mere fancy – and provided a profound, if unsystematic, exposition of the new epistemology and aesthetic.

For the Romantics, then, the imagination served an integrating function in a world divided by the accelerating declension of shared philosophical, religious, and moral assumptions. The individual became the inspired locus for an intuitive perception of the spiritual forms and energies that invested the otherwise fragmented phenomenal world with an exalted coherence, a significance at once immediate and ultimate. For Wordsworth and Coleridge, Blake and Shelley, Emerson and Whitman, the imagination was elevated from the image-making talent of the Neoclassicists into the sublime human faculty, one through which the perceiving subject penetrated to the essential reality and transcendental interrelatedness of the objects of experience.

This Romantic synthesis, however, was an ideal unstable from the outset – precariously conceived and only sporadically achieved. Because everything depended upon the metamorphic, mutually completing encounter between subject and object, the Romantic ideology made the highest claims for, and put the highest demands upon, individual vision outside the traditional religious and social institutions. When, under the stress of such an extreme and ultimate test, the individual failed to achieve or to sustain the visionary moment, the very basis for meaning in personal and social life was shaken: Consciousness felt itself severed from self and world. Romanticism thus contained in its vaunting claims of synthesis the seeds of its own dissolution. The threat of dissolution was present almost from the start, accelerated through the Victorian period, and seemed to play itself out in fin de siècle aestheticism. As a result, intellectuals and artists of the twentieth century found the efficacy of both intuition and reason perilously undermined, just when they faced a political upheaval so dire and far-reaching that civilization itself seemed threatened. Out of that apocalyptic sense, which was to lend Spengler's *Decline of the West* its prophetic aura, Modernism defined itself as the meta-ideology of the twentieth century, in response to and opposition to Romanticism. Stevens and Williams considered the chief challenge to the Modernist poet – one of life-or-death urgency – to be the redefinition of the function of the imagination, liberating it from shaky epistemological premises and so reclaiming its power in the face of psychological and social circumstances more desperate than the Romantics or the Victorians, for all their prescience, had foreseen.

Stevens had a contemplative, speculative turn of mind, whereas Williams' scientific empiricism made him genuinely indifferent to, even impatient with, philosophizing. As Modernists, both knew that the argument for the imagination could not rest on metaphysical or mystical claims about the source and ends of its operation. For them, and for most of their contemporaries, it could only be construed in human and naturalistic terms. Yet neither Stevens nor Williams was a rationalist; both postulated and strove to substantiate a creative imagination superior to fancy, or to the image-making talent of the Neoclassicists, for both felt that its discriminations and connections determined the quality of our personal and collective lives.

The Modernists thus assigned to creativity a different origin and end than did the Romantics. The twentieth-century poet became less the recipient than the agent of perception: Discriminations had to precede connections, and only analysis yielded provisional reconstruction. The deformity or formlessness of modern life required decreation as a condition for creation, reduction as the prerequisite for invention. The calculated wildness of Williams' evocation of these dual aspects of the imagination in *Spring and All* (1923) represents his attempt to recapture the dionysian rapture of the Romantics for his own post-Nietzschean, Modernist purposes: "The imagination, intoxicated by prohibitions, rises to drunken heights to destroy the world. Let it rage, let it kill. The imagination is supreme. . . . Then at last will the world be made anew."[8] The completion of the work, as anticipated in the last sentence, carries Williams past the anarchism of Dada and Futurism into a recreative effort closer to Cubism, an effort that must be sustained from moment to moment: "To refine, to clarify, to intensify that eternal moment in which we alone live there is but a single force – the imagination. . . . Yes, the imagination, drunk with prohibitions, has destroyed and recreated everything afresh in the likeness of that which it was."[9]

In Williams' view the imagination which abstracts things "from ordinary experience" does not forfeit "close identity with life": The circuit completes and objectifies itself in the artifact, whose integrity comprises "some approximate co-extension with the universe." The poem, therefore, repudiates "plagiarism after nature" – the futile attempt at realism – to achieve something much more challenging and consequential: a reality not opposed to nature but "apposed to it."[10] In its apposition to nature the verbal construct serves to mediate the epistemological schism between subject and object:

> In great works of the imagination A CREATIVE FORCE IS SHOWN AT WORK MAKING OBJECTS WHICH ALONE COMPLETE SCIENCE AND ALLOW INTELLIGENCE TO SURVIVE – his picture lives anew. It lives as pictures only can: by their power TO ESCAPE ILLUSION and stand

between man and nature as saints once stood between man and the sky – their reality in such work, say, as that of Juan Gris.[11]

The artist pieces together connections from fragments, makes form from chancy associations, brings consciousness to bear on objects alien to his consciousness, and thereby composes in a lifetime of poetry his relation to the world, his place in it, his passage through it. As art, his life choices – selections and rejections – take shape and direction, the lens of the artist's "personality" providing the terms and limits within which its "creative force" perceives and invents.[12]

Wallace Stevens' temper was epicurean where Williams' was dionysian:

> It is the *mundo* of the imagination in which the imaginative man delights and not the gaunt world of the reason. The pleasure is the pleasure of powers that create a truth that cannot be arrived at by reason alone, a truth that the poet recognizes by sensation. The morality of the poet's radiant and productive atmosphere is the morality of the right sensation.[13]

Nevertheless, for Stevens too sensation is not just a passively received impression but an actively and accurately achieved response. Stevens is just as clear as Williams about the Cubist conviction that "modern reality is a reality of decreation": "When Braque says 'The senses deform, the mind forms,' he is speaking to poet, painter, musician and sculptor." And they are equally clear that against a "violent" reality the imagination must itself be a powerful counterforce, exerting "a violence from within that protects us from a violence without."[14]

Thus for Stevens, as for Williams, the "truth" of poetry is a function of the poet's personality. "The imagination of a man disposed to be strongly influenced by his imagination" abstracts and translates elements from reality into his chosen medium, yet this abstract arrangement generates a sense, however illusory, of "an agreement with reality, . . . which he believes, for a time, to be true, expressed in terms of his emotions or, since it is less of a restriction to say so, in terms of his personality." The fastidious convolutions and qualifications of this characteristic statement prepare us for Stevens' stoic admission that "the difference between philosophical truth and poetic truth appears to be final." "A High-Toned Old Christian Woman" begins with the famous dictum, "Poetry is the supreme fiction, madame"; the poem proceeds to dispel the sense of bathetic deflation by affirming the "supreme fiction" as comparable to the old woman's religious hypotheses. Stevens' retort to the charges of political irrelevance from the Marxists and of decadent hedonism from moralists like Yvor Winters remained resolute. "The power of the mind over the possibilities of things," "pressing back against the pressure of reality," provides the means of "self-preservation" which "enables us to perceive the normal in the abnormal, the opposite of chaos in chaos"; the imaginative fiction, even if illusory, "help[s] people to live their lives" and gives "life whatever savor it possesses."[15]

2

Stevens' and Williams' remarks on the imagination provide a consise summary of Modernism as a literary term. For both, the poet is not the individual locus of vision, the inspired medium who sees into the life of things and tries to find adequate language for his mystical experience, as the Romantics had maintained. The poet is instead an individual through whose personality the "constructive faculty" of the imagination strives to compose the fragments of impression and response into an autotelic art-object. Anti-idealist and antimystical, the poet does not reveal the divinity of Nature but invents an apposite, aesthetic coherence, necessarily less than absolute in extrinsic terms but, ideally, self-sustained in its own medium. In Stevens' characteristic phrasing, "our revelations are not the revelations of belief, but the precious portents of our own powers." The repetition of "revelation" subverts religious faith; the percussive alliteration emphasizes the metamorphic imagination.[16]

Nevertheless, the common allegiance of the two poets to Modernism served to reveal equally defining tensions between them. Different temperaments and personalities made them testy about and jealous of each other, and they kept a safe distance. Despite the promises and invitations in their correspondence, they saw each other seldom and were not personally intimate. As early as the "Prologue" to *Kora in Hell*, Williams lampooned "dear fat Stevens, thawing out so beautifully at forty," "a fine gentleman . . . who has suddenly become aware of his habits and taken to 'society' in self-defense . . . immaculately dressed."[17] Each nervously fretted about the other's productivity and reputation. To a publisher, Stevens lamented: "Williams, I believe, writes every day or night or both, and his house must be full of manuscript, but it is quite different with me." Complaining directly to Williams in 1925 about the heavy responsibilities of job and family, Stevens openly envied Williams, just back from Europe with a lengthening list of published books, but then offered Williams a nasty explanation of his productivity: "But then your imagination has always exploited your fellow-townsmen and the chances are that you don't mind it."[18] Williams' irritation at the Stevens letter quoted in *Kora* should have warned him against asking Stevens to introduce his *Collected Poems* a decade later: The result was to rankle him for the rest of his life. More and more, neither read the other's work. Stevens resolutely resisted addressing *Paterson,* and Williams confessed to Marianne Moore that he was encountering increasing trouble muddling through Stevens' later, longer meditations.[19] At the same time that Stevens was writing to Williams, "You deserve everything that is coming your way" – and, in his way, meaning it – he was also confiding to his friend Barbara Church that Williams seemed "a man somehow disturbed at the core and making all sorts of gestures and using all sorts of figures to conceal it from himself." When Williams' stroke kept him from appearing with Stevens at the Bard convocation, Stevens responded to a standing ovation at the end of the ceremonies with a remark to his host on the platform: "Well, we didn't need the old man after all, did we?" (He did make amends with a tender letter to Williams the next day.)[20]

They were right to feel uneasy with each other at a level below that of their real and mutual respect: Their differences were matters of substance as well as ego and illustrate an ambiguity within their common Modernist aesthetic. This was clear from the Stevens letter in the *Kora* "Prologue"; Stevens explained in a postscript that he had decided to send Williams the letter reluctantly, because "it is quarrelsomely full of my own ideas of discipline." He charges Williams with dissipating his energies and obscuring his voice through his stubborn refusal to develop "a fixed point of view" and "a single manner or mood": "To fidget with points of view leads always to new beginnings and incessant new beginnings lead to sterility."[21] Williams' dismissive response was the sneering caricature of dear fat Stevens, but he continued from time to time to acknowledge, with a mixture of insecurity and resentment, Stevens' "sophisticated, urbane voice" measuring out its elegant pentameters.[22] For his own part, toward the end of his life, Stevens hailed the younger Richard Eberhardt as a poet "right in my own way of thinking of things, although I am not too sure that my own way of thinking of things is right, particularly when I come across the universal acceptance of Bill Williams, for instance, who rejects the idea that meaning has the slightest value and describes a poem as a structure of little blocks."[23] In the same year (1953) Stevens sniffed to Barbara Church: "If the present generation likes the mobile-like arrangements of line to be found in the work of William Carlos Williams or the verbal conglomerates of e. e. cummings, what is the next generation to like? Pretty much the bare page, for that alone would be new."[24]

When Williams called Stevens "his most worthy American contender,"[25] it was obviously a real contention, and though each fretted that the other had won greater acceptance and so won the contest, neither wavered in his way of "thinking of things" and giving them utterance. The precise terms of their contention deserve the closest attention because their efforts to reclaim the imagination from the ruins of Romanticism derived from significantly different literary and epistemological assumptions. Where Williams found himself sharing Pound's Imagist principles, Stevens spoke as a representative of the Symboliste tradition coming into English. As a result they found themselves at cross-purposes about the function of the imagination as a translator of experience into language. When Williams chose his stateside compatriot over his transatlantic friend and competitor to introduce his *Collected Poems,* his miscalculation taught him which was the poetic compatriot and which the poetic competitor. The more reserved Stevens had told Williams that he was reluctant to write the introduction, but Williams persisted and thus precipitated a long-postponed engagement of their dispute, revealing a schism, or at least an irresolution, at the heart of Modernism.

The adjectives with which Stevens labeled Williams' work caused understandable offense: "romantic," "sentimental," "antipoetic," "realist."[26] Stevens suggested that Williams vacillated between his sentimental proclivities (which, for example, exploited his fellow townsmen) and his antipoetic, realist, "Imagist" side. Williams did not balk at the Imagist tag. (Pound had quickly recognized Williams and Marianne Moore as the most interesting exemplars of Imagist principles among the poets "exiled" in the home country.) But Stevens' discussion seemed to define Imagism as an antipoetic realism – precisely the opposite of Williams' argument in *Spring and All.* Stevens also considered Marianne Moore to be antipoetic, realist, and Imagist, but less baldly so than Williams. The key word was "romantic," which Stevens must have known was a red flag to a *soi-disant* antiromantic like Williams. What could Stevens mean by calling him a twentieth-century romantic? Stevens himself supplied a curious answer:

> What, then, is a romantic poet now-a-days? He happens to be one who still dwells in an ivory tower, but who insists that life would be intolerable except for the fact that one has, from the top, such an exceptional view of the city dump and the advertising signs of Snider's Catsup, Ivory Soap and Chevrolet Cars; he is the hermit who dwells alone with the sun and the moon, but insists on taking a rotten newspaper.[27]

The problem with Stevens' description of the romantic as idealistic solipsist in a shabby, commercialized society is that it befits him more than Williams. It is Stevens who would write "The Man on the Dump" from an ivory tower elevation that permitted the exotic figurations and highfalutin language of that poem. Williams, never as reclusive as Stevens, would choose to squat on the dump, reading the rotten Paterson or Rutherford newspaper.

Stevens' review of Marianne Moore's *Selected Poems,* written the next year, formulates more coherently what he was fumbling toward in the Williams introduction. Commending Moore with the title, "A Poet That Really Matters," Stevens distinguishes between good and bad forms of romanticism. Invoking Irving Babbitt, that rabid antiromantic, Stevens associates "romantic in the derogatory sense" with the attempt to treat ordinary objects ("things, like garden furniture or colonial lingerie or, not to burden the imagination, country millinery") as "strange, unexpected, intense, probable, superlative, extreme, unique, etc." Stevens' supercilious inventory of objects is calculated to prejudge as palpably silly the imaginative effort to romanticize the world of everyday objects and events, much less to transfigure the Paterson of billboards, urban waste, and daily news. Stevens' "Man Whose Pharynx Was Bad" found that "the malady of the quotidian" rendered him voicelss and verseless. On the other hand, the review goes on to cite A. E. Powell's *The Romantic Theory of Poetry* to help define "romantic in its other sense," the sense that he wishes to praise in Moore, as the poet's ability "to reproduce for us the feeling as it lives within himself."[28]

A reading of the Williams introduction against the Moore review, then, pegs Williams as "romantic in the derogatory sense" and Moore as "romantic in its other sense." The Moore whom Stevens praises for rendering internal states of feeling may be hard to reconcile with the poet who insisted on real toads in her imaginary gardens, and who described things – ostrich, skunk, snail, katydid – with a scrupulously observant eye. Even the poem entitled "The Mind Is an Enchanting Thing" fixes the mind on precise discriminations of phenomena. In describing Moore as a reflection of himself, Stevens was trying to reclaim her from Williams' side of their poetic argument.

The underlying issue was Imagism as a mode of poetic perception and expression, and Stevens was initially hesitant to state his discontent with Imagism openly. The following statement masks the grounds of his complaint:

> Imagism . . . is not something superficial. It obeys an instinct. Moreover, it is an ancient phase of poetry. It is something permanent. Williams is a writer to whom writing is the grinding of a glass, the polishing of a lens by means of which he hopes to be able to see clearly. His delineations are trials. They are rubbings of reality.[29]

Much less trusting than Williams that rubbings from reality made for clear sight, or for that matter for sight of anything he would take comfort in seeing, Stevens found an alternative for his discomfort in the aestheticism of Pater and Santayana (whom he knew at Harvard) and in the Symbolisme of Mallarmé and Valéry. Symbolisme and Imagism proved to be the most important and long-lasting influences in modern poetry precisely because they assumed dialectical roles within Modernist poetics. The polarity was recognized from the outset. Pound sometimes gave *Imagisme* its French spelling in order to designate the new movement as a critique of and an alternative to Symbolisme. Amy Lowell admonished the fledgling John Gould Fletcher that he had to choose between her Imagist direction and the mood-symphonies of his friend Conrad Aiken.

Lowell's warning was a maneuver in poetic politics. Symbolisme and Imagism developed as polar aspects of poetic Modernism following the disintegration of the Romantic synthesis of subject and object. Thus while Modernism constitutes on one level an overt and programmatic rejection of Romanticism, it constitutes on another level an extension of the epistemological issues that the decadence of Romanticism precipitated. In terms of the subject–object split, Imagism represents the attempt to render the objects of experience, Symbolisme the attempt to render subjective psychological and affective states. The first mode finds affinities with the visual arts in using language and shaping the poem on the page as ideogram; the second moves towards suggestive imprecision in metaphor and associative language and relies heavily on auditory and musical effects.

Admittedly these two large and diverse movements should not be contrasted dichotomously. After all, Pound stated as the first and basic premise of Imagism the "direct treatment of the 'thing,' " whether subjective or objective," thus admitting the rendering of a subjective "thing" as a type of image.[30] And Stevens, for his part, kept reminding himself that the imagination must maintain a relation to – even if possible suggest an agreement with – the world outside the mind, kept insisting that metaphorical and rhythmic fictions must periodically be dumped on the trash heap of a recalcitrant and unillusioned reality. Faced with a polarity between subject and object, we must try to accommodate both terms; and under that pressure the terms tend to slip in and out of one another. Nonetheless, the underlying and defining inclination of the Imagist imagination – a phrase which in this context is *not* redundant – is to fix the mind and its language on the phenomena of experience; the corresponding inclination of the Symboliste imagination is to dissolve sense impressions into linguistic evocations of psychic states. Even the converse effort – that is, an Imagist rendering of a psychological state as a subjective "thing," or a Symboliste evocation of a natural object – underscores, rather than undermines, this distinction. For example, a juxtaposition of Pound's "The Jewel Stair's Grievance" or Williams' "Flowers by the Sea" with Stevens' "Thirteen Ways of Looking at a Blackbird" or "Sea Surface Full of Clouds" reinforces the impression that Imagism operates by project-ing mind and medium to engage things, whereas Symbolisme absorbs things into mind and medium. In the one case consciousness commits subject to object; in the other, consciousness commits object to subject.

As we have seen, the Modernist in Williams joined Stevens in distin-guishing the art-object from the objects of nature as autotelic in the words or stone or pigment and canvas that constitute its only existence: "The word must be put down for itself, not as a symbol of nature but a part, cognizant of the whole – aware – civilized."[31] Yet his apposition of the art-object to nature is not as extreme as Stevens' notion of a violent opposition, of art "against" nature. For Williams, the art-work is not symbolic of nature, as Romantic metaphysics claimed; yet it assumes a place in nature – apart yet a part, an act of consciousness that is, or strives to be, "cognizant of the whole."

In fact, even in the "Preface" to *Spring and All,* perhaps his most com-batively Modernist work, Williams saw the imagination working out of "close identity with life" to produce something that is an "approximate co-existence with the universe." The imagination decreates so that "at last the world will be made anew."[32] That prophetic claim could be read to mean that the world is made anew only as the artificial recreation of the art-work. But Williams postulated the possibility that the art-work would mediate the gap between subject-world and object-world. In standing "between man and nature as saints once stood between man and the sky," the imaginative work reconstitutes "everything afresh" *not* in its own image but "in the likeness of that which it was." Conscious-ness makes a difference for the objects of consciousness; it summons them to and invests them with a significance that Williams could at times sug-gest was their intrinsic significance. The imagination, not God or Nature, is the source and agent of meaning, but for that reason it is bent not on transforming but on revealing the object:

> Understood in a practical way, without calling upon mystic agencies, of this or that order, it is that life becomes actual only when it is identified with ourselves. When we name it, it exists. . . . My whole life has been spent (so far) in seeking to place a value upon experience and the objects of experience.[33]

One Stevens essay, first presented to the English Institute in 1948, offers his own version of "Imagination as Value." It provides a counterstatement not only to such Williams passages as the one above, but also to his own "Rubbings of Reality" essay (1946) concerning Williams' Imagism and to his essay, also from 1948, "About One of Marianne Moore's Poems." There Stevens speaks of Moore's imaginative stance and verbal strategies as deriving from "contact with reality as it impinges upon us from outside, the sense that we can touch and feel a solid reality which does not wholly dissolve itself into the conceptions of our own minds."[34] That epistemological conviction is the underlying premise of Imagism, and by recognizing it in Moore, Stevens in effect retracts his earlier attempt to claim her as a kind of Symboliste.

That epistemological conviction, however, is one that Stevens did not share. In "Imagination as Value" he reiterated his conviction that such an attitude was "romantic" and sentimentally exploitative: "We must somehow cleanse the imagination of the romantic. . . . The romantic belittles it. The imagination is the liberty of the mind. The romantic is a failure to make use of that liberty. It is to the imagination what senti-mentality is to feeling."[35] In fact, "Imagination as Value" draws out the consequences of the Symboliste premise that "we live in the mind." For "if we live in the mind, we live with the imagination" – not, admittedly, Coleridge's and Emerson's "imagination as metaphysics" but Mallarmé's and Valéry's "imagination as a power of the mind over external objects, that is to say, reality." Stevens is repeating his earlier distinction between imaginative modes, but without the arguable distinction between good and bad romanticism. Moreover, while an unillusioned, unapolo-getic acknowledgment of the mind's "power . . . over the possibilities of things" might seem to make for sentimental exploitation, it can instead be seen to preclude that Imagist weakness, because in the Symboliste mode "what is engaging us . . . has nothing to do with the external world." At that point, the poet becomes an agnostic idealist: "The Pla-tonic resolution of diversity appears. The world is no longer an extra-neous object, full of other extraneous objects, but an image. In the last analysis, it is with this image of the world that we are vitally con-cerned."[36]

But is the vital concern for an "image of the world," or for the "world of the image"? The inversion of the grammatical subordination in the phrase creates a subtle but critical epistemological distinction. Williams or Pound or Moore tend to think of the poem as an "image of the world." But the "world of the image" is a more accurate phrase to describe Ste-vens' concern – or, in his own phrase, "the *mundo* of the imagination," for "a poet's words are of things that do not exist without the words."[37] Stevens prefers the risks of escapism to those of romantic realism. His Symboliste aestheticism made him, like Santayana, a skeptical Platonist, while Williams and Pound, Moore and H.D., believed in their different kinds of empiricism — for Pound and H.D., in fact, an empiricist Platonism.

3

A reading of those poems in which Stevens and Williams directly engage each other substantiates in practice their theoretical differences. "Nuances of a Theme by Williams"[38] appeared in *Harmonium* in 1923, but dates from 1918, the year of Stevens' admonitions about Williams' undeveloped viewpoint in the *Kora* "Preface." Stevens' "Nuances" reprints Williams' brief early piece, "El Hombre," and rewrites it at greater length, reducing the four lines of Williams to a subtext.

"El Hombre" addresses a terse, austere apostrophe to a star, so understated that it must use an exclamation point to provide concluding emphasis:

> It's a strange courage
> you give me, ancient star:
>
> Shine alone in the sunrise
> toward which you lend no part!

Addressing a star is an instance of the so-called pathetic fallacy — a time-honored convention for expressing intense empathy with the observed object. Except for the underlying association of man and star in the title, Williams employs no figurative language. The colon makes the transition between couplets: the second couplet specifies the life-and-death courage that the speaker draws from the star's persistent, solitary shining in, and despite, the overwhelming light of the rising sun. The irony of the poem lies in the recognition that the cyclic process of nature, renewed each dawn, dooms both star and man.

Stevens' poem fastens on two phrases, "shine alone" and "lend no part," and provides elaborate glosses:

> I
> Shine alone, shine nakedly, shine like bronze,
> that reflects neither my face nor any inner part
> of my being, shine like fire, that mirrors nothing.
>
> II
> Lend no part to any humanity that suffuses
> you in its own light.
> Be not chimera of mourning,

> Half-man, half star.
> Be not an intelligence,
> Like a widow's bird
> Or an old horse.

Stevens rejects the pathetic fallacy as an appropriation of brute nature by human consciousness, which denigrates it to the romanticized and sentimentalized status of kept beast or pet: "Like a widow's bird / or an old horse." Star is all and only star, not "half-man"; subject and object share no mirroring correspondence, as the Romantics had claimed.

On the surface, Stevens' strategy might appear anti-Symboliste here, refuting Williams' own practice with an Imagistic insistence on the object stripped of human attribution. But, whatever the argument of the poem, the quality of its language betrays Stevens' Symboliste allegiances. The incantatory repetitions and rhythms, the proliferation of metaphors and similes, create an opaque verbal atmosphere, obscuring the central fact that "El Hombre" renders with immediacy: the star's lone shining and waning in the dawn. Williams' language eschews metaphoric indirection to focus consciousness on the object; Stevens' language indulges in metaphor to establish its fictive and self-referential independence of the object.

The last poem in Stevens' *Collected Poems*, "Not Ideas about the Thing but the Thing Itself,"[39] seems more explicitly than "Nuances" to proclaim, via Williams, an Imagist viewpoint. But again, its manner makes the psychological difference between the two poets all the clearer:

> At the earliest ending of winter,
> In March, a scrawny cry from outside
> Seemed like a sound in his mind.
>
> He knew that he heard it,
> A bird's cry, at daylight or before,
> In the early March wind.
>
> The sun was rising at six,
> No longer a battered panache above snow . . .
> It would have been outside.
>
> It was not from the vast ventriloquism
> Of sleep's faded papier-mâché . . .
> The sun was coming from outside.
>
> That scrawny cry – it was
> A chorister whose c preceded the choir.
> It was part of the colossal sun,

Surrounded by its choral rings,
Still far away. It was like
A new knowledge of reality.

The poem recounts the mind's coming to consciousness of a winter world
verging towards spring – a favorite subject of Williams, the most famous
treatment of which is perhaps "By the road to the contagious hospital."
Here Stevens' winter scene is not described but suggested through two
elements, the bird-cry and the sun, drawn into affiliation by the waking
mind. The poem follows the process through which the disembodied
bird-cry seems to take on increasing objectivity through association with
the dawning sun. At first the cry "seemed like a sound in the mind." But
by the third tercet the sun, "rising at six," "would have been outside,"
and by the end of the next tercet "was coming from outside." In the
expanded possibilities suggested by the enjambment of the final tercets,
the cry "was part of the colossal sun, // Surrounded by its choral rings."
The repeated pronoun "it," referring sometimes to the cry and sometimes to the sun, comes in the last sentence to include both, and by implication everything else, within the sun's radiant circumambience: "It was
like / A new knowledge of reality."

At the same time, however, the sunrise becomes in the course of the
poem not just the thing observed but itself a metaphor for the process by
which consciousness becomes aware of the thing observed: "He knew
that he heard" the bird and saw the sun. The self-circling, self-defining
repetition of words and imagery – increasingly characteristic of late Stevens – enacts the gradual clarification and expansion of the impression in
the mind. Objects are absorbed into metaphor, and the metaphor of dawn
becomes the verbal construct itself: The words are the dawning.

Williams' rendering of "the earliest ending of winter"[40] allows a revealing
comparison:

By the road to the contagious hospital
under the surge of the blue
mottled clouds driven from the
northeast – a cold wind. Beyond, the
waste of broad, muddy fields
brown with dried weeds, standing and fallen

patches of standing water
the scattering of tall tress

All along the road the reddish
purplish, forked, upstanding, twiggy
stuff of bushes and small trees

with dead, brown leaves under them
leafless vines –

Lifeless in appearance, sluggish
dazed spring approaches –

They enter the new world naked,
cold, uncertain of all
save that they enter. All about them
the cold, familiar wind –

Now the grass, tomorrow
the stiff curl of wildcarrot leaf
One by one objects are defined –
It quickens: clarity, outline of leaf

But now the stark dignity of
entrance – Still, the profound change
has come upon them: rooted, they
grip down and begin to awaken

Like Stevens, Williams traces the mind's awakening to spring's awakening; but in this instance consciousness is almost totally absorbed into the scene, attendant upon and attendant to natural process. The meticulous accuracy of the details confirms Williams' negative capability (his early fascination with Keats strengthened his inclination to subject ego to object), and dramatizes the contrast to Stevens' absorption with the lovely tracings of the mind's watching itself watching in words. Williams' poem, rather than Stevens', exemplifies the Imagist dictum, "Not Ideas about the Thing but the Thing Itself."

Something different transpires through Stevens' widening verbal sweeps, climaxing in the last two tercets, the only enjambed tercets in the poem. Here, as in other Stevens poems ("Mrs. Alfred Uruguay," for example), sunrise is the figure for the advent of the imagination to the world: not the false, weak, merely decorative, "romantic" imagination of moonlight or half-light – dismissed in this poem by means of the self-indicting rhetoric of "a battered panache above the snow" and "the vast ventriloquism / Of sleep's faded papier mâché" – but the virile imagination that demonstrates the mind's power over the possibilities of things. Despite the title of the poem, its first and last concern is with the mind itself rather than with the thing itself.

Consider the difference between "One by one objects are defined – / It quickens" and "It was like / A new knowledge of reality." The Williams poem obliquely acknowledges the lens of consciousness toward the end through the intrusion of abstract words like "clarity," "the stark dignity of entrance," "the profound change," but the abstractions feel earned by their grounding in specification. Aside from the personification in "sluggish, / dazed spring approaches," there is not a single figure of speech in the poem. The Stevens poem, by contrast, begins and ends with a simile; the bird cry which at first only "seemed like a sound in the mind" does become in the course of the poem a sound in the mind: "like a new knowledge of reality." That "like" at opening and close, sealing the poem in simile, is the signature of the Symboliste, as opposed to the Imagist, imagination.

A third pair of poems reverses the roles of the two poets, this time with Williams reacting to and against Stevens. "Description without Place"[41] might well have been one of those ruminative poems that Williams told Moore he found more and more befuddling. It was included in *Transport to Summer* (1947), the volume that also contained "Esthétique du Mal" and "Notes toward a Supreme Fiction," but Williams read it first in its original journal publication and "didn't like [it] at all."[42] What's more, Williams took personal affront at what he took to be a caricature of him in the following lines:

> the hard hidalgo
> Lives in the mountainous character of his speech;
>
> And in that mountainous mirror Spain acquires
> The knowledge of Spain and of the hidalgo's hat –
>
> A seeming of the Spaniard, a style of life,
> The inventor of a nation in a phrase.

Williams did not explain why he took the hard hidalgo as a portrait of him (aside, presumably, from his Spanish blood and middle name), or why he took offense. But he threw himself into writing "A Place (Any Place) to Transcend All Places" in rebuttal.

It is easy to see why Williams would have rejected Stevens' delicately delineated meditation on the interplay of seeming and being, metaphor and thing, fictions and actualities. But, unlike "Nuances of a Theme by Williams" and "Not Ideas about the Thing but the Thing Itself," "Description without Place" makes no recognizable nod to Williams, not even in the disguise of the "hard hidalgo" (despite Williams' reaction). The theme and diction are *echt* Stevens, as in the penultimate section:

> Description is revelation. It is not
> The thing described, nor false facsimile.

> It is an artificial thing that exists,
> In its own seeming, plainly visible,
>
> Yet not too closely the double of our lives,
> Intenser than any actual life could be,
>
> A text we should be born that we might read,
> More explicit than the experience of sun
>
> And moon, the book of reconciliation,
> Book of a concept only possible
>
> In description, canon central in itself,
> The thesis of the plentifullest John.

The poem, then, describes a fictive concept, existent only in the medium in which it is contrived, as superior to any place of reference. But this book of revelation, unlike St. John's, does not reconcile us to earth or heaven, but draws us into its own ambience. Against such conceptualizing Williams argued furiously that a place (any place, as long as it was the poet's place) is the ground of thought and speech; his title proclaims the particular as transcendent. A catalogue of details locates the poet in New York; and although the poem as a whole lacks the shapeliness of Williams' best work, the following lines exemplify in an image from nature his dictum "no ideas but in things":

> leaves filling,
> making, a tree (but
> wait) not just leaves,
> leaves of one design that
> makes a certain design,
> no two alike, not like
> the locust either, next in line,
> nor the Rose of Sharon, in
> the pod-stage, near it – a
> tree! Imagine it! Pears
> philosophically hard.

The pear tree, its individual leaves "no two alike," is distinguished from the adjacent locust and Rose of Sharon; such a "design" of particulars is the only kind of philosophical knowledge Williams will admit.

As for the Spanish hidalgo, Williams was being unnecessarily defensive; there is no reason to suppose that Stevens had him in mind. In fact, a reading of those lines in the context of the conclusion to "Description without Place" identifies the hidalgo not as Williams in masquerade but, on the contrary, as the Stevensian hero of capable imagination:

Thus the theory of description matters most.
It is the theory of the word for those

For whom the word is the making of the world,
The buzzing world and lisping firmament.

It is a world of words to the end of it,
In which nothing solid is its solid self.

As, men make themselves their speech: the hard hidalgo
Lives in the mountainous character of his speech;

And in that mountainous mirror Spain acquires
The knowledge of Spain and of the hidalgo's hat –

A seeming of the Spaniard, a style of life,
The invention of a nation in a phrase,

In a description hollowed out of hollow-bright,
The artificer of subjects still half night.

It matters, because everything we say
Of the past is description without place, a cast

Of the imagination, made in sound;
And because what we say of the future must portend,

Be alive with its own seemings, seeming to be
Like rubies reddened by rubies reddening.

Nevertheless, Williams' rising to the challenge he thought that Stevens was slyly presenting serves to dramatize again the contrary – in some fundamental ways even contradictory – positions of the Imagist and the Symboliste. The still unsettled dialectic between the two most influential and long-lasting movements in modern poetry has sought to resolve an ambiguity in the philosophic and linguistic assumptions of Modernism itself. The choice between "pears / philosophically hard" and "rubies reddened by rubies reddening" has again and again been blurred or fuzzed over, sometimes deliberately; but some version of that choice has persistently presented itself whenever fundamental questions have arisen about what the artist sees and says. On the one hand, Williams says, "The eyes by this / far quicker than the mind"; to which Stevens replies, "Description is / Composed of a sight indifferent to the eye."[43] The very elusiveness of the terms – subject and object, mind and nature – makes discriminations about their interaction in the language of the poem all the more difficult, and all the more necessary.

NOTES

1 *The Letters of Wallace Stevens,* ed. Holly Stevens (New York: Knopf, 1966), p. 228.
2 *Letters,* p. 589.
3 *Letters,* p. 665.
4 *Letters,* p. 768.
5 Paul Mariani, *William Carlos Williams: A New World Naked* (New York: McGraw-Hill, 1981), pp. 498–99; *Selected Letters of William Carlos Williams,* ed. John C. Thirlwall (New York: McDowell, Obolensky, 1957), p. 229.
6 *The Autobiography of William Carlos Williams* (New York: Random House, 1951), p. xii.
7 Mariani, *William Carlos Williams,* pp. 630–31.
8 William Carlos Williams, *Spring and All,* in *Imaginations,* ed. Webster Schott (New York: New Directions, 1970), pp. 90–91.
9 *Imaginations,* pp. 89, 93.
10 *Imaginations,* pp. 110, 111, 105, 121.
11 *Imaginations,* p. 112.
12 *Imaginations,* pp. 105, 107, 112.
13 Wallace Stevens, *The Necessary Angel: Essays on Reality and the Imagination* (London: Faber and Faber, 1951), pp. 57–58.
14 *The Necessary Angel,* pp. 175, 161, 26, 36.
15 *The Necessary Angel,* pp. 54, 136, 36, 153, 30.
16 *The Necessary Angel,* pp. 164, 175.
17 *Imaginations,* pp. 15, 27.
18 *Letters,* pp. 271, 245.
19 *Selected Letters of William Carlos Williams,* p. 305.
20 *Letters,* pp. 589, 592; Mariani, *William Carlos Williams,* p. 630.
21 *Imaginations,* p. 15.
22 Mariani, *William Carlos Williams,* p. 499.
23 *Letters,* p. 803.
24 *Letters,* pp. 800–801.
25 Mariani, *William Carlos Williams,* p. 498.
26 Wallace Stevens, *Opus Posthumous,* ed. Samuel French Morse (New York: Wallace Stevens, Knopf, 1957), pp. 254, 255, 256.
27 *Opus Posthumous,* p. 256.
28 *Opus Posthumous,* p. 251.
29 *Opus Posthumous,* p. 258.
30 Ezra Pound, *Literary Essays of Ezra Pound,* ed. T. S. Eliot (New York: New Directions, 1954), p. 3.

31 *Imaginations,* p. 102.
32 *Imaginations,* pp. 101, 105, 111, 91.
33 *Imaginations,* pp. 115–16.
34 *The Necessary Angel,* p. 96.
35 *The Necessary Angel,* p. 138.
36 *The Necessary Angel,* pp. 136, 140, 141, 151.
37 *The Necessary Angel,* pp. 57–58, 32.
38 Wallace Stevens, *The Collected Poems of Wallace Stevens* (New York: Knopf, 1954), p. 18.
39 *Collected Poems,* p. 534.
40 *Imaginations,* pp. 95–96.
41 *Collected Poems,* pp. 339–346.
42 William Carlos Williams, *The Collected Later Poems of William Carlos Williams* (New York: New Directions, 1963), pp. 113–15; Mariani, *William Carlos Williams,* p. 824.
43 Williams, *Collected Later Poems,* p. 114; Stevens, *Collected Poems,* pp. 343–44.

2

Stevens without Epistemology

GERALD L. BRUNS

> I shall whisper
> Heavenly labials in a world of gutturals.
> It will undo him. (CP 7)

The word "epistemology" in my title is to be taken loosely to mean a concern for how the mind links up with reality. The question I want to ask is this: What happens to our reading of Stevens' poetry when the problem of how the mind links up with reality is no longer of any concern to us?

Let me try to clarify this question by situating Stevens' work within the following history of conceptual changes: (1) There was a time when questions about nature, reality, or the world began to be reformulated as questions about the mind, consciousness, or imagination rather than as questions about God. This was the "epistemological turn" in Western thinking when (beginning, say, with Descartes) Mind or Spirit replaced Being as the "metaphysical centrum" of reality.[1] (2) Then there came a time when questions about mind or consciousness (and therefore also questions about reality) began to be reformulated as questions about language. This was the "linguistic turn," sometimes identified with the slogan, "There is nothing outside of language," but which can be interpreted in different ways depending upon how one stands with respect to a number of modern intellectual traditions (analytic philosophy of language, Heideggerian phenomenology, structuralism and its aftermath, and so on). (3) Finally, there came a time when questions about language (and also therefore questions about mind and reality) began to be reformulated as questions about social practice, or about historically contingent, socially determined, and ideologically bound conventions of human life: questions, in short, about how people get on with one another in particular human situations when they must get something done, or settled, or answered, or when something otherwise engages more than one person. This was the "hermeneutical turn," where hermeneutics means something more than methods of textual interpretation or textual reception. Hermeneutics here means philosophical hermeneutics and is concerned with the historical and dialogical nature of understanding – that is, with the temporal, social, and political conditions in which human understanding goes on.[2]

We know that it is quite natural to situate Stevens' work within an idealist framework. The epistemological turn, whereby the mind is all in all, is foundational for Stevens and is presupposed by the entire tradition of Stevens criticism. It is also possible to read Stevens within the context of the linguistic turn – but not so easy: I tried to do this ten years ago in unblinking defiance of the fact that language just didn't have much reality for Stevens (it's simply another mental product).[3] In order to read Stevens in this way one must map onto his work the outlook or vocabulary of someone like the later Husserl or the later Heidegger – or, if one prefers, then Derrida. J. Hillis Miller is perhaps the best-known critic to have situated Stevens in the context of the linguistic turn, chiefly by exploiting the epistemological skepticism (if that is what it is) of Stevens' later poetry.[4] It is interesting how the word "later" keeps turning up here: It's a way of marking the turn in the road produced by an epistemological crisis (falling out of faith with the mind), or by persuasion to the idea that there really *is* nothing outside of language – that the linguisticality of human existence, as Heideggerians like to say, makes talk about imagination and reality sound prehistoric, like talk about God. We know what it is like to read Stevens when we no longer believe in God. What is it to read him when you no longer believe that there is such a thing as the imagination?

The issue here is the distancing factor that conceptual change introduces into the reading of poetry. There is an important way in which Stevens' poetry has receded into history, leaving us behind (perhaps without our knowing it, since our own historicality is frequently what we don't know). My question is this: What happens when one reads Stevens' poetry from the standpoint made available by the hermeneutical turn in human thinking? Let me try to give some sense of what an answer to this question might sound like. (There are a number of answers to this question, and Stevens criticism ought to be in the business of testing them.)

From a hermeneutical standpoint the main problem for Stevens is not how the mind links up with reality but what to do about other people.

This is not a problem of knowledge or of language (that is, it is not a problem of how language links up with reality); rather it is a problem of dialogue, of speech that presupposes and even engages the discourse of other people. In current jargon, it is a problem of alterity rather than one of intersubjectivity. (Intersubjectivity is a notion that enables us to integrate other minds into the idealist framework.) It is true that the problem of others is not something that Stevens addresses in any explicit way (at least not at first glance). His poetry will always be a poetry of the spectator, in which the main thing is to see something or to construct something, and thereby to count it as knowable or intelligible or valuable (or, in short, something to call one's own). What Stevens is after is something against which to strike attitudes and to have experiences. Stevens' poetry is a poetry of world-making in which "the tongue is an eye" and the eye is a "silent rhapsodist."[5] The tongue is meant for experience rather than for discourse, as much for tasting as for talk; and the ear is a "secondary" sense (CP 374), especially when we are encouraged, as we almost always are, to listen for sounds that cannot actually be heard. A good conversation for Stevens is going to be a "Continual Conversation with a Silent Man" (CP 359), which is no doubt why we never learn what Ramon Fernandez has to say about "the glassy lights" that master the night and portion out the sea (CP 130). It is not, as Hugh Kenner once remarked, that there are no people in Stevens' poetry[6] (Stevens critics are testy about having their man called a solipsist); it is that people in Stevens' poetry never answer back.

I think that Stevens would have understood very well what I'm getting at. One of the "Adagia" reads as follows: "Life is an affair of people not of places. But for me life is an affair of places and that is the trouble." (OP 158) We ought to have an opinion as to what this trouble is.

It should be stressed that the trouble here is not quite the same as the problem of other minds, a famous topic in analytic philosophy. However, the problem of other minds is a way of converting epistemology into a question of language, and eventually (by way of the later Wittgenstein) into a question about social reality.[7] For example, instead of asking about the existence of the world, we ask about what is not empirically available but nevertheless *there* in ways we can't account for. How can we know (for certain) that other minds exist, or that someone who says she is in pain is really in pain, or that the sign "S" corresponds to the sensation "S" when someone not ourselves cries out "S"? The answer is that we cannot know in any logically justifiable sense of "know," although we can usually judge well enough to get along with, or do right by, someone who seems to be in pain. We can even manage to come to terms with someone who happens to be faking it. The problem here is social rather than epistemological. Or, as Stanley Cavell says, epistemological problems are real problems, but they are problems about other people and not just problems about how the mind links up with reality.[8]

In the poetry of Stevens, however, the problem of others is more directly related to the uncanny power that voices have over us, and why we sometimes cannot abide them. At any rate, for Stevens the problem of others often takes the form of what to do about strange, unwanted, discordant, or uncontrollable voices. Stevens says, "When the mind is like a hall in which thought is like a voice speaking, the voice is always that of someone else." (OP 168) What can we say about such a voice?

Naturally when we hear such a voice (sounding as if in a hallway or a corridor of our own heads) we want to be able to say where it comes from, because being able to identify its source will be a way of getting rid of it, and we want to be rid of it. We know what it is to hear such a thing, and it's always frightening, because the voice, after all, isn't coming from anywhere: It's just there where it doesn't belong. It is our old nemesis, the disembodied voice, the voice out of nowhere, the voice of the other or the outsider that has now somehow got inside us, sounding where our own voice ought to be. We can neither objectify this voice nor appropriate it, nor can we close ourselves off to it (the way we can to unwelcome sights); it is the voice sounding at night or in darkness, and often it can simply mean that things are going to pieces:

> No lamp was burning as I read,
> A voice was mumbling, "Everything
> Falls back to coldness,
>
> Even the musky muscadines,
> The melons, the vermilion pears
> Of the leafless garden." (CP 147)

In a poetry of world-making this sort of voice is inimical. The best we can do is to assimilate its antithetical character by calling it "apocalyptic."

A good place to engage this theme is with Crispin's experience in "The Comedian as the Letter C":

> Here was the veritable ding an sich, at last,
> Crispin confronting it, a vocable thing,
> But with a speech belched out of hoary darks
> Noway resembling his. (CP 29)

Much of Stevens' poetry is designed to keep Crispin's experience of otherness from happening: For Stevens, success in experience means hearing no one's voice but your own. One can then enter into a new world without any loss of self-possession:

> Out of my mind the golden ointment rained,
> And my ears made the blowing hymns they heard.
> I was myself the compass of that sea:
>
> I was the world in which I walked, and what I saw
> Or heard or felt came not but from myself;
> And there I found myself more truly and more strange.   (CP 65)

However, this experience (this monologue of world-making) is not just yours for the having. It requires you to silence the voice of the other by appropriating it (if you can) into your own interior discourse, as in "Two Figures on a Dense Violet Night," which sounds at first like a love poem but is really nothing of the sort:

> Be the voice of night and Florida in my ear.
> Use dusky words and dusky images.
> Darken your speech.
>
> Speak, even, as if I did not hear you speaking,
> But spoke for you perfectly in my thoughts,
> Conceiving words,
>
> As the night conceives sea-sounds in silence
> And out of their droning sibilants makes
> A serenade.   (CP 86)

It would be easy to multiply examples of this appropriation of the voice of the other by a discourse of the self that is in turn characterized as a monologue or song of world-making. Think of how often the metaphors of the choir and the chorus turn up in Stevens' poetry – rings of men, for example, chanting "Their boisterous devotion to the sun" (CP 70). Stevens has many ingenious ways of silencing the "crackling of voices in the mind" (CP 292) by converting such sound into an ideal form that cannot be comprehended except by visual analogies, or by analogies with a soundless music reverberating in an ideal chamber, or by recourse to some figure of transcendence like the "central man," "a mirror with a voice, the man of glass, / Who in a million diamonds sums us up" (CP 250). "Owl's Clover," arguably Stevens' most political poem, is rich in conversions of this sort:

> There each man
> Through long cloud-cloister-porches, walked alone,
> Noble within perfecting solitude,

Like a solitude of the sun, in which the mind
Acquired a transparence and beheld itself
And beheld the source from which transparence came;
And there he heard the voices that were once
The confusion of men's voices, intricate
Made extricate by meanings, meanings made
Into a music never touched to sound. (OP 54)

Remember what happens to that great metaphor of human social life in 'Of Modern Poetry'': "Then the theatre was changed / Into something else" (CP 239). To be sure, the theater (or, in its converted state, poetry) "has to be living, to learn the speech of the place." It presupposes other people – "It has to face the men of the time and to meet / The women of the time. It has to think about war" – but only in order to subsume these public things into "something else," something more private, inward, and purely poetic:

                                  It has
To construct a new stage. It has to be on that stage
And, like an insatiable actor, slowly and
With meditation, speak words that in the ear,
In the delicatest ear of the mind, repeat,
Exactly, that which it wants to hear, at the sound
Of which, an invisible audience listens,
Not to the play, but to itself, expressed
In an emotion as of two people, as of two
Emotions becoming one. (CP 240)

This conversion of public dialogue and social interchange into private meditation, and of people into pure emotion, seems to me to summarize my whole point.

Don't misunderstand me, however. I'm not talking simply about Stevens' conservatism, or his well-known resistance to social and political themes, or his intolerance of historical reality. I'm talking about "the delicatest ear of the mind" and what it refuses to hear, or what it represses. Two references may help to clarify things. The first is to Mikhail Bakhtin, whose critique of the monological attitude is well known. In an essay translated in *The Dialogical Imagination,* "Discourse and the Novel," Bakhtin characterizes human discourse as a conflict between two forces, one that seeks "to unify and centralize the verbal-ideological world" in a single "unitary language" or authoritative monologue, the other that disperses discourse into a "heteroglossia," or what Bakhtin calls the "dialogized heteroglossia," in order to emphasize the constant give and take, back talk, and cross-purposes among the multiple and frequently incommensurable language-games that make up human speech. Language in the world is structured like a conversation rather than like a grammar. It is the many-layered discourse of contrary voices in diverse tongues, each expressing its own "socio-ideological" outlook, its own temporal horizon, its own special history. It is not, as logic, linguistics, and the philosophy of language would have it, a system that makes possible the endless creative production of sentences.[9] It was Bakhtin's view that poetry is on the side of logic and defines itself in relation to the pole of unitary language; it requires the silencing of heterogeneous voices – in contrast to the novel, which is heteroglot in its very structure. Stevens' "The Novel" is a wonderful comic illustration of this idea:

> The sun stands like a Spaniard as he departs,
> Stepping from the foyer of summer into that
> Of the past, the rodomontadean emptiness.
>
> *Mother was afraid I should freeze in the Parisian hotels.*
> *She had heard of the fate of an Argentine writer. At night,*
> *He would go to bed, cover himself with blankets –*
>
> *Protruding from the pile of wood, a hand,*
> *In a black glove, holds a novel by Camus. She begged*
> *That I stay away.* These are the words of José. . . .
>
> He is sitting by the fidgets of a fire,
> The first red of red winter, winter-red
> The late, least foyer in a qualm of cold.
>
> How tranquil it was at vividest Varadero,
> While the water kept running through the mouth of the
>   speaker,
> Saying: *Olalla blanca en el blanco,*
>
> Lol-lolling the endlessness of poetry.
> But here the tranquillity is what one thinks.
> The fire burns as the novel taught it how.   (CP 457–58)

One can read "The Novel" as a parody of how a novel sounds, and also as a corresponding celebration of the sounds a noble rider makes ("How tranquil it was at vividest Varadero"). And one can compare this to "Certain Phenomena of Sound," in which music appropriates the story that Redwood Roamer has to tell and turns the Roamer himself from a tale spinner into a transcendental ego:

> So you're home again, Redwood Roamer, and ready
> To feast . . . Slice the mango, Naaman, and dress it

With white wine, sugar and lime juice. Then bring it,
After we've drunk the Moselle, to the thickest shade

Of the garden. We must prepare to hear the Roamer's
Story . . . The sound of that slick sonata

Finding its way from the house, makes music seem
To be a nature, a place in which itself

Is that which produces everything else, in which
The Roamer is a voice taller than the redwoods,

Engaged in the most prolific narrative,
A sound producing the things that are spoken.   (CP 286–87)

– or, in other words, another monologue of world-making.

As Bakhtin contends, "The poet is a poet insofar as he accepts the idea of a unitary and a singular language and a unitary, monologically sealed-off utterance." (DI 296) Plainly, however, Bakhtin's thesis presupposes a formalist poetics and, more generally, a European outlook that contrasts sharply with much of American poetic practice. *Spring and All, The Waste Land* ("He Do the Police in Different Voices"), *The Cantos* – to give only obvious examples – are heteroglot poems. "A poem can be made out of anything," Williams said, even newspaper clippings.[10] No need to repeat here Stevens' antivernacular sentiments, inspired by Williams' poetics; the poetry is made of these sentiments in any case:

A few final solutions, like a duet
With the undertaker: a voice in the clouds,

Another on earth, the one a voice
Of ether, the other smelling of drink,

The voice of ether prevailing, the swell
Of the undertaker's song in the snow

Apostrophizing wreaths, the voice
In the clouds serene and final, next

The grunted breath serene and final,
The imagined and the real, thought

And the truth, Dichtung und Wahrheit, all
confusion solved, as in a refrain

One keeps on playing year by year,
Concerning the nature of things as they are.   (CP 177)

"The world of poetry," Bakhtin says, "no matter how many contradictions and insoluble conflicts the poet develops within it, is always illumined by one unitary and indisputable discourse. Contradictions, conflicts, and doubts remain in the subject, in thoughts, in living experiences – in short, in the subject matter – but they do not enter the language itself. In poetry, even discourse about doubts must be cast in a discourse that cannot be doubted" (DI 286). Thus it is not surprising that even the deconstructive Stevens of the late poems – the Stevens of J. Hillis Miller and Joseph Riddel, for whom ground turns into figure and back again, leaving the reader of two minds about everything – holds fast against dialogue to the attitude of soliloquists, rhapsodists, choristers, and trees shouting in unison:

> The trees have a look as if they bore sad names
> And kept saying over and over one same, same thing,
>
> In a kind of uproar, because an opposite, a contradiction,
> Has enraged them and made them want to talk it down.
>
> (CP 522)

My second reference is to the last chapter of Geoffrey Hartman's *Saving the Text*, "Words and Wounds," in which Hartman speaks of the "ear-fear" that closes contemporary criticism off to the voice and to the power of the word to wound us (and perhaps also to heal or cure us) when we hear it – that is, when we open ourselves to it in an active listening.[11] Yet listening is not easy, because listening cuts against our modern norms of rationality. Hartman wants to recover the old idea that poetry is thaumaturgical – capable of wounding or curing in the way that curses and benedictions once did – but this requires that we learn to read it with a "conscious ear" (p. 141). The difficulty is that in reading this way we put ourselves at risk, for we expose ourselves to alterity. "When the mind is like a hall in which thought is like a voice speaking, the voice is always that of someone else": *that* is the experience of alterity. Stevens, it appears, knew it well – and liked it not at all.

Hartman's theme is the "vulnerability of the ear" (pp. 123–36), and his thinking on this point shows the influence of Emmanuel Levinas, for whom the "saying" that occurs in dialogue is more than simply "a modality of cognition" – that is, more than simply the conveying of information with a view toward subsequent decoding by anyone who happens along. Dialogue does not consist in an exchange of views or a contest between them; rather, it consists "in the uncovering of oneself, in sincerity, the breaking up of inwardness and the abandon of all shelter, exposure to traumas, vulnerability."[12] Dialogue means the loss of subjectivity (a terrible loss for an idealist, since this means the loss of self, world – everything). Hartman pursues this line of thinking as part of his ongoing quarrel with formalism and, in particular, with the structuralist devaluation of *parole* in favor of *langue* – its attempt to replace mystery with system, dispelling the otherness with which every utterance resonates.

In "Words and Wounds," however, Hartman introduces the notion of the voice and its unsettling power over us expressly to undo a puzzle in Derrida's thinking, namely the connection that Derrida makes between speech and metaphysics. In Derrida's celebrated declaration of "the death of speech" and the beginning of writing as the end of a "metaphysics of presence" one can see the resurgence of ancient anxieties about the voice that Enlightenment dreams of a philosophical language were meant, among other things, to dispel.[13] (A philosophical language is one in which everything can be expressed exactly and which therefore requires no interpretation.) Derrida's early writings look like a powerful critique of the idea of a philosophical language – deconstruction looks like a critique of structuralism – but the odd thing, as Leibniz and Bishop Wilkins knew in the seventeenth century, is that this is a language which can only be written: whence its power, that is, its ability to free itself from equivocation or to produce sentences whose meaning is determined by logical form rather than by situations of use. All modern theories of language (saving perhaps Heidegger's) presuppose this notion of language and the writing which, so to speak, underwrites it.

Writing represses, displaces, or demystifies the phenomenon of voice in order to emancipate us from bondage to divine or demonic presences, and it is in accord with this emancipation, or as part of its ideology, that we obtain our Enlightenment norms of rationality – single-mindedness, univocity, agreement with reality (or the next best thing, freedom from illusion, the knowledge that our fictions are only fictions), reflexivity, clarity of perception, self-certainty, orderly progress, hierarchical construction, and so on. Jack Goody has spelled out this idea in *The Domestication of the Savage Mind,* in which he argues that literacy is specifically productive of the critical attitude that makes philosophical thought possible.[14] To put it plainly, writing is foundational for philosophy; or as Stanley Cavell says, it is foundational for philosophy of a certain systematic sort, namely formal philosophy or philosophy of the schools: logic, epistemology, and metaphysics – philosophy, in other words, from which a good deal gets excluded, including (Cavell says) the better part of the American tradition, including Emerson, for example, and Thoreau. (In the graduate schools of philosophy Emerson and Thoreau draw black stares.) It is, Cavell says, "quite as if repressing Emerson's thought were an essential responsibility of professional philosophy."[15] Emerson and

Thoreau are heteroglot philosophers at odds (in a way that C. S. Peirce is not) with the idea of a philosophical language; they are the strange, unwelcome, unsettling voices that philosophy requires be silenced.

Cavell finds very puzzling "Derrida's sense, or intuition, that bondage to metaphysics is a function of the promotion of something called voice over something called writing; whereas for me it is evident that the reign of repressive philosophical systematizing – sometimes called metaphysics, sometimes called logical analysis – has depended upon the suppression of the human voice."[16] Hartman's reading of Derrida's *Glas* – a collage of texts by Hegel and Genet played off against one another by Derrida's punning commentary – reveals the source of Cavell's puzzlement about Derrida and how it may be resolved. Derrida may speak of the privileging of voice and the marginality of writing; but in order to make sense of him, one must see how his thinking turns inside out, or doubles back. What he has done in *Glas* is to compose a text on behalf of the death of philosophical language and the return of repressed voices (the voice of Genet, for example – for who is Genet to enter into a dialogue with the monumental Hegel?). *Glas* is nothing if not heteroglot. Following Cavell's insight and Hartman's line of thought, one could call *Glas* the closest thing in French to an American text, where an American text is that which is animated by alien voices – strange, unwelcome, unsettling voices that fail to cohere into a chorus. Hartman's word for such a feature is "glossolalia," or speaking in tongues – originally a sacred, now also a poetic gift.[17]

Stevens does not, it appears, compose American texts. Indeed, it has been remarked often enough (by Hugh Kenner, for one) that Stevens composes the closest thing in English to French texts – texts which, as in the case of Mallarmé, repress the phenomenon of voice in favor of *écriture*.[18] Sound in such a text aspires not to the illusion of someone speaking but to the formal conditions of music. Think, for example, of the character of sounds in Stevens' verse; a score of dissertations have made the point that Stevens' ears are tuned to exotic noise:

> In Hydaspia, by Howzen,
> Lived a lady, Lady Lowzen,
> For whom what is was other things.   (CP 272)

Such sounds have been constructed as objects of aesthetic interest, making no claim upon anything but our contemplative ear; they are sounds which do not require us to answer, sounds which we do not actually have to hear:

> Tell *X* that speech is not dirty silence
> Clarified. It is silence made still dirtier.
> It is more than an imitation for the ear.

He lacks this venerable complication.
His poems are not of the second part of life.
They do not make the visible a little hard

To see nor, reverberating, eke out the mind
On peculiar horns, themselves eked out
By the spontaneous particulars of sound.

We do not say ourselves like that in poems.
We say ourselves in syllables that rise
From the floor, rising in speech we do not speak.   (CP 311)

Which poet could be more easily substituted for the poet X – Mallarmé
or William Carlos Williams?

What is interesting about Stevens – and perhaps this is *his* strange,
difficult way of being an American poet – is the way in which he plays
out again and again, the drama of the fear and repression of alien voices.
I have said that Stevens' poetry will always be a poetry of the spectator,
where the main thing is to see something. But the point I have been
making is that he is a poet troubled by the sort of poetry he is *not* writing
and perhaps can't bring himself to think of *as* poetic – the poetry of the
other, disturbing our monumental slumber. This is the context in which
I like to read "The Course of a Particular," with its ambiguous cry of
the leaves:

Today the leaves cry, hanging on branches swept by the wind,
Yet the nothingness of winter becomes a little less.
It is still full of icy shades and shapen snow.

The leaves cry . . . One holds off and merely hears the cry.
It is a busy cry, concerning someone else.   (OP 96)

Of all the sounds in Stevens' verse, the cry might be said to have a special
character because it so often betokens otherness, as in "Not Ideas about
the Thing but the Thing Itself," in which "a scrawny cry from outside /
Seemed like a sound in his mind" (CP 534). In any event, the characteristic movement is to convert otherness into aesthetic identity, whence
the "scrawny cry" proves after all to be simply "A chorister whose c
preceded the choir" (CP 534) – not something alien, but rather a
momentary dissonance, an unsynchronized sound. So, in "The Course
of a Particular," the poet finally concludes that the cry we have heard is
nothing to be alarmed about: It is not a "human cry" (OP 96), and certainly not a divine one, but only leaves making their normal eerie sound:

It is the cry of leaves that do not transcend themselves,

> In the absence of fantasia, without meaning more
> Than they are in the final finding of the ear, in the thing
> Itself, until, at last, the cry concerns no one at all.   (OP 96–97)

Or, in other words, in its "final finding" the poet's ear has dispelled its fear, but only by making familiar the otherness of the cry that initiates the poem. When "One holds off and merely hears the cry" – that is, when one simply listens – one is open to the voice of "someone else"; it is only by converting to "the delicatest ear of the mind" that one can conclude, as the poet does conclude, that "the cry concerns no one at all."

The counterstatement of the epistemologist would be that all I've been saying is just willful misreading, since plainly a poem like "The Course of a Particular" is what it has always been said to be: namely, a poem about the act of the mind vis-à-vis a certain phenomenon of sense. Nothing "repressive" is going on in the poem; rather, the "conversion" that I imagine taking place is simply the mind's normal work in making poetry possible. In this case the poem's obvious point is that poetry is not always possible – not, for example, in "the nothingness of winter," when the mind and its phenomena just don't come together. Otherness, in other words, reduces to disharmony:

> And though one says that one is part of everything,

> There is conflict, there is a resistance involved;
> And being part is an exertion that declines:
> One feels the life of that which gives life as it is.   (OP 96)

In short, the poem is a well-known poem of decreation and (more important) demystification:

> The leaves cry. It is not a cry of divine attention,
> Nor the smoke-drift of puffed-out heroes, nor human cry.
>
> (OP96)

That is what leaves sound like in "the absence of fantasia" (OP 97): they sound like leaves!

I want to stress that there is nothing wrong with this orthodox reading. On the contrary, it is entirely consistent with the poem in question precisely in the sense that readings within an epistemological framework serve to reinforce the outlook that Stevens strives in poem after poem to preserve. My point is that the phenomenon of the voice of the other always threatens this outlook, and that this is the truth that Stevens' poetry teaches us, particularly in the way in which otherness is obsessively aestheticized:

Here in the North, late, late, there are voices of men,
Voices in chorus, singing without words, remote and deep,
Drifting choirs, long movements and turning sounds,

And in a bed, in one room, alone, a listener
Waits for the unison of the music of the drifting bands
And the dissolving chorals, waits for it and imagines

The words of winter in which these two will come together.
(OP 90)

More than this, however, I have tried to make my point in a way that questions the Americanness of Stevens' texts – given the absence from his poetry of anything remotely resembling the heteroglossia that, I would argue, otherwise characterizes much of American writing. I want to conclude by saying that this questioning would not have surprised or dismayed Stevens at all. A poem that illustrates this point very well is "Autumn Refrain," which contrasts the European nightingale and the American grackle, the literary and the vernacular, the written and the spoken, purity and disruption:

The skreak and skritter of evening gone
And grackles gone and sorrows of the sun,
The sorrows of sun, too, gone . . . the moon and moon,
The yellow moon of words about the nightingale
In measureless measures, not a bird for me
But the name of a bird and the name of a nameless air
I have never – shall never hear. And yet beneath
The stillness of everything gone, something resides,
Some skreaking and skrittering residuum,
And grates these evasions of the nightingale
Though I have never – shall never hear that bird.
And the stillness is in the key, all of it is,
The stillness is all in the key of that desolate sound.   (CP 160)

The poem is organized as a sonnet: (1) A grackle, let us say, is a blackbird meant to be looked at, not to be heard; but in this country *that* is just what one must listen to, as against the melancholy song of the nightingale. To American ears, filled with the vernacular racket of grackles, the nightingale is just a word in a poem by Keats ("The yellow moon of words about the nightingale"). Our most poetic experience, in contrast to Keats', is of the silence of departed grackles. (2) In "Autumn Refrain" the "skreaking and skrittering" of the grackles yields to the pure poetic measures of the nightingale – but notice that this displacement almost fails. Even after the grackles have gone, leaving the poet alone to medi-tate the poem he cannot hear, "something resides, / Some skreaking and skrittering residuum" that "grates these evasions of the nightingale." (And so we may speak once more of the return of the repressed.) (3) As always, however, the heteroglossia is appropriated by a unitary language; the mental echo left by the grackles is harmonized, or poetized. It is taken up in the last two lines, at any rate, by a music that only "the delicatest ear of the mind" could hear, namely, the nightingale's melancholy song: "The stillness is all in the key of that desolate sound." True poetry is of the mind; it is antivernacular – "speech we do not speak" (CP 311). It is like the difference between "clickering" (CP 28) and "immaculate" (CP 188) syllables. "Skreaking and skrittering," like the "gibberish of the vulgate" (CP 397) – this is the world we hear, until, like the man on the dump, we manage (if we can) to find our own voice:

> One sits and beats an old tin can, lard pail.
> One beats and beats for that which one believes.
> That's what one wants to get near. Could it after all
> Be merely oneself, as superior as the ear
> To a crow's voice? Did the nightingale torture the ear,
> Pack the heart and scratch the mind? And does the ear
> Solace itself in peevish birds? Is it peace,
> Is it a philosopher's honeymoon, one finds
> On the dump? Is it to sit among mattresses of the dead,
> Bottles, pots, shoes and grass and murmur: *aptest eve:*
> Is it to hear the blatter of grackles and say
> *Invisible priest;* is it to eject, to pull
> The day to pieces and cry *stanza my stone?*
> Where was it one first heard the truth? The the.   (CP 202–203)

The "blatter of grackles" – the voice of the other – is the speech of the unmade world.[19]

NOTES

1   See Kenneth Schmitz, "Toward a Metaphysical Restoration of Natural Things," in *An Etienne Gilson Tribute,* ed. Charles O'Neil (Milwaukee: Marquette University Press, 1959), pp. 245–52.

2   The starting point for this line of thinking would be Martin Heidegger, *Being and Time,* trans. John Macquarrie and Edward Robinson (New York: Harper and Row, 1962); see especially p. 206: "We can make clear the connection of discourse with understanding and intelligibility by considering an existential possibility which belongs to talking itself – hearing. . . . Hearing is constitutive for discourse. . . . Listening to . . . is Dasein's existential way of Being-open as Being-with for Others. Indeed, hearing constitutes the

primary and authentic way in which Dasein is open for its ownmost poten-
tiality-for-Being – as in hearing the voice of the friend whom every Dasein
carries with it." This theme of listening and otherness emerges in an interesting way in analytic philosophy in Donald Davidson, "Thought and Talk,"
in *Truth and Interpretation* (Oxford: Clarendon Press, 1984), p. 157: "A creature cannot have thoughts unless it is an interpreter of the speech of another."

3   Gerald L. Bruns, *Modern Poetry and the Idea of Language* (New Haven: Yale
    University Press, 1974), pp. 220–31.
4   J. Hillis Miller, "Stevens' Rock and Criticism as Cure," *The Georgia Review*
    30 (Spring/Summer 1976), 5–31, 330–48.
5   The first phrase is from Wallace Stevens, *Opus Posthumous,* ed. Samuel French
    Morse (New York: Knopf, 1957), p. 167; hereinafter cited as OP. The sec-
    ond phrase comes from *The Collected Poems of Wallace Stevens* (New York:
    Knopf, 1954), p. 259; subsequently cited as CP.
6   Hugh Kenner, *A Homemade World* (New York: William Morrow, 1975), p.
    75.
7   See David Bloor, *Wittgenstein: A Social Theory of Knowledge* (New York:
    Columbia University Press, 1983), pp. 50–82.
8   Stanley Cavell, *The Claim of Reason: Wittgenstein, Skepticism, Morality, and
    Tragedy* (Oxford: Oxford University Press, 1979), pp. 329–496.
9   Mikhail Bakhtin, *The Dialogical Imagination,* trans. Michael Holquist (Aus-
    tin: University of Texas Press, 1982), pp. 270–75. Hereinafter cited as DI.
    See Kenner, *A Homemade World,* pp. 74–75, where he says of Stevens' verse:
    "There is a great deal of language in these poems, with no one speaking it
    except the grave impersonal voice of poetry, and there is little variety of
    feeling. The most that happens is that the voice turns whimsical. That grave
    equable voice, as dispassionate as *things,* weaves its whimsical monologue;
    Crispin and Mrs. Pappadopoulos and Mrs. Alfred Uruguay and other
    improbable folk are nodes in the monologue."
10 William Carlos Williams, *Kora in Hell: Improvisations,* in *Imaginations,* ed.
    Webster Schott (New York: New Directions, 1970), p. 70.
11 Geoffrey Hartman, *Saving the Text* (Baltimore: Johns Hopkins University
    Press, 1981), pp. 123–26.
12 Emmanuel Levinas, *Otherwise than Being or Beyond Essence,* trans. Alphonso
    Lingis (The Hague: Martinus Nijhoff, 1981), p. 48.
13 Jacques Derrida, *Of Grammatology,* trans. Gayatri Chakravorty Spivak (Bal-
    timore: Johns Hopkins University Press, 1976), p. 8.
14 Jack Goody, *The Domestication of the Savage Mind* (Cambridge: Cambridge
    University Press, 1977), pp. 36–51.
15 Stanley Cavell, "Politics as Opposed to What?" in *The Politics of Interpreta-
    tion,* ed. W. J. T. Mitchell (Chicago: University of Chicago Press, 1983), p.
    185.
16 Cavell, "Politics as Opposed to What?", p. 197. I've discussed this matter
    of writing and voice in "Writing Literary Criticism," *The Iowa Review* 12
    (Fall 1981), 34–42.
17 See Hartman, *Saving the Text,* p. 122: "To avoid the misunderstanding that

mine is a 'postcritical' theory like Paul Ricoeur's in *The Symbolism of Evil*, I exclude religious and magical views [of spoken words], though they are always implied."

18   See Bruns, *Modern Poetry and the Idea of Language*, pp. 101–17, on the Mallarmé text.

19   Compare the following from "Credences of Summer":

> Fly low, cock bright, and stop on a bean pole. Let
> Your brown breast redden, while you wait for warmth.
> With one eye watch the willow, motionless.
> The gardener's cat is dead, the gardener gone
> And last year's garden grows salacious weeds.
>
> A complex of emotions falls apart,
> In an abandoned spot. Soft, civil bird,
> The decay that you regard: of the arranged
> And of the spirit of the arranged, *douceurs,*
> *Tristesses,* the fund of life and death, suave bush
>
> And polished beast, this complex falls apart.
> And on your bean pole, it may be, you detect
> Another complex of other emotions, not
> So soft, so civil, and you make a sound,
> Which is not part of the listener's own sense.   (CP 377)

3

Revolving in Crystal:
The Supreme Fiction and
the Impasse of Modernist Lyric

MARJORIE PERLOFF

December 23, 1941. In response to a request from Katharine Frazier of the small private Cummington Press in Massachusetts, Stevens writes:

> . . . provided you are not in too much of a hurry, it is possible that I might be able to do some things for you during the winter and spring, say between now and the end of June.[1]

And here is Stevens a week later (December 30), Miss Frazier having sent him some sample Cummington books:

> Somehow your package looks like the packages that used to come from the Cuala Press. I expect to enjoy looking over it this evening. In the meantime, you can count on me for something, but not earlier than the end of June, unless I should have some luck.[2]

Stevens was true to his word. By May 14, 1942, he had informed the Cummington Press that his manuscript would be ready within the month and that its title would be *Notes toward a Supreme Fiction:*

> There will be 30 poems, each of seven verses, each verse of three lines. In short, there will be 21 lines of poetry on each page.
>   These thirty poems are divided into three sections, each of which constitutes a group of ten. There will be a group title, but the separate poems will not have separate titles. . . . Each of the three groups will develop, or at least have some relation to, a particular note: thus the first note is . . .
>
>   I
>   IT MUST BE ABSTRACT
>   The second note is

41

II

IT MUST CHANGE

Both of these sections are completed and I am now at work on the third section, the title of which is . . .

III

IT MUST GIVE PLEASURE.

These are three notes by way of defining the characteristics of supreme fiction. By supreme fiction, of course, I mean poetry. (L 406–407)

On June 1, he writes Miss Frazier that "the manuscript of *Notes* is in the mail" (L 408).

I begin with this bit of publishing history because it is all too customary to read *Notes toward a Supreme Fiction* as if it arose from the sea of spuming thought *ex vacuo* – a Poem that took the Place of a Mountain, a noble work that is not only Stevens' finest, but perhaps the great long poem of the twentieth century (so posits Frank Kermode); or the culmination of the Romantic tradition (Helen Vendler); or the most brilliant of the belated crisis-poems written in the tradition of Emerson and Whitman (Harold Bloom); or, most recently, a forerunner of Derrida, whose terminology it uncannily anticipates (Joseph Riddel).[3] Commentaries on the *Notes* – and they are legion – are painstaking in their zeal to explain what it is, line by line, canto by canto, that Stevens' poem is *saying* (or not saying). The poem's political and social context, on the other hand, is rarely mentioned, an odd state of affairs when one considers that *Notes* is, to paraphrase Yeats, a meditation in time, not of civil, but of world war. It is, to be more precise, a kind of antimeditation, fearful and evasive, whose elaborate and daunting rhetoric is designed to convince both poet and reader that, despite the daily headlines and radio bulletins, the real action takes place in the country of metaphor. For, as Stevens put it in one of his "Adagia," "Reality is a cliché from which we escape by metaphor. It is only *au pays de la métaphore qu'on est poète.*"[4]

What was the reality-as-cliché to be escaped in the winter of 1942? Here a short list of dates may serve as a reminder:

September 1, 1939	Hitler's invasion of Poland and, two days later, England and France's declaration of war on Germany.
April 1940	The end of the so-called phony war (or "winter of illusion" as Churchill called

	it) with Hitler's annexation of Scandinavia.
May 1940	Hitler's invasion of the Netherlands.
June 15, 1940	The fall of France: Hitler invades Paris and Vichy regime is set up in the South.
September 1940	The Battle of Britain: air destruction of Coventry, Birmingham, etc.
September 27, 1940	Tripartite Pact: Japan joins European Axis.
June 22, 1941	Hitler's invasion of the Soviet Union and consequent dissolution of the Nazi–Soviet pact.
December 7, 1941	Pearl Harbor.
December 11, 1941	Germany and Italy's declaration of war on U.S.
January 12, 1942	U-Boat offensive begins off coast of Cape Cod. The so-called Torpedo Curtain: U.S. ships sunk as close as 30 miles from New York City.
April 1, 1942	Battle of Bataan, with heavy American losses.
May 7–8, 1942	Battle of the Coral Sea, which frustrates Japanese offensive against New Guinea and, indirectly, Australia.
June 4, 1942	Battle of Midway, which marks end of defensive phase of Pacific War. Great U.S. victory.
July 25, 1942	Decision of Allies to invade North Africa as gateway to Europe.

Stevens' response to such events can be traced most fully in his correspondence, particularly the correspondence with Henry Church that began early in 1939 when Church, then coediting with Jean Paulhan the Paris review *Mesures,* wrote to Stevens requesting permission to publish translations of some of the *Harmonium* poems. A wealthy American expatriate, Church was living at Ville D'Avray outside Paris with his second wife, Barbara, who was German. There is nothing in his letters to Stevens that suggests unusual insight or intellect; he appears, on the contrary, to have been a fairly typical dilettante, interested in as much art, music, literature, and philosophy as the good life might absorb – a kind of Burbank with a Baedeker.[5] For Stevens, however, Church became something of an alter ego – the well-bred, cultured American (his mother, to Stevens' delight, had been born in Hartford, Connecticut) at home in the European art world. In January 1942, Stevens writes to Church: "I love to hear from you. You have so thoroughly lived the life that I should be glad to live." (L 401) Before long he had decided to dedicate the *Notes* to him. No doubt one of Church's particular appeals for Stevens – like that of his Ceylonese correspondent, the minor poet and translator Leonard van Geyzel – was that he had no involvement with the New York literary establishment, which was at that time heavily left-wing. To Church, Stevens could express his views on poetry and politics quite openly. On June 1, 1939, for example, he writes:

> What counts, I suppose, is one's relation to contemporary ideas. Much of that, however, would be irrelevant as part of an introduction to a group of poems obviously having nothing to do with the ideas of the day in which they were written, nor of today. I am, in the long run, interested in pure poetry. No doubt, from the Marxian point of view this sort of thing is incredible, but pure poetry is rather older and tougher than Marx and will remain so. My own way out toward the future involves a confidence in the spiritual role of the poet. (L 340)

Ironically, the "ideas of the day" so seemingly beside the point vis-à-vis "pure poetry" and "the spiritual role of the poet" were to prove only too decisive for Henry Church himself. On a visit to America in September 1939, when the Nazis took Poland, the Churches felt it too dangerous to return to Paris. Indeed, they did not return until the war was over in 1946. For the Churches, American exile (in New York, Princeton, and Arizona) meant primarily an interruption of their normal art world activities. The two problems discussed at great length in the correspondence with Stevens are (1) what to do with *Mesures,* and (2) whether and how to endow a poetry chair and a series of poetry lectures at Princeton. On October 11, 1940, Stevens writes to Church that such a chair might cost between ten and twenty thousand dollars, but that the cost would be worthwhile, for "you might well have in return something that would make you forgetful of the loss of Paris" (L 375). Note that the "loss of Paris" is here (as elsewhere in the letters) regarded as Henry Church's personal loss, not as anything larger. Stevens became so excited about the notion of the poetry chair that he drew up an entire job description and curriculum:

What is intended is to study the theory of poetry in relation to what poetry has been and in relation to what it ought to be. For this purpose, poetry means not the language of poetry but the thing itself, wherever it may be found. It does not mean verse any more than philosophy means prose. The subject-matter of poetry is the thing to be ascertained. (L 377)

The notion that poetry has a special subject matter is one to which I shall return. For the moment, I merely want to note that Stevens, in articulating what is essentially a romantic faith in "the thing itself," regularly takes a defensive, perhaps somewhat petulant posture:

> . . . if it be objected that this [the view of poetry as special discourse] is carrying humanism to a point beyond which it ought to be carried in time of so much socialist agitation, the answer must be that humanism is one thing and socialism another. (L 378)

"Socialist agitation," one might think, is a rather odd way of referring to the then-ongoing Battle of Britain or to the occupation of his beloved France, but for Stevens the ruling principle is *aesthetic detachment*. As he was to put it to Hi Simons the following year: "About social obligation: It is simply a question of whether poetry is *a thing in itself* or whether it is not. I think it is." (L 403)

The poetry series, in any case, materialized, and Stevens agreed to participate in it. By January 9, 1941, he tells Church, "I know pretty definitely what my paper will be about" (L 384); by February a first draft has been written (L 386); and the lecture itself, "The Noble Rider and the Sound of Words," was delivered on May 8.[6] Before we turn to this essay, which is in many ways a prose counterpart to the *Notes*, let us trace some further political motifs that run through the letters to Church. Asked to recommend some critics who might contribute to *Mesures*, Stevens writes (January 9, 1941):

> The news about *Mésures* has the right sound. There are at the present time a good many Europeans over here. I should suppose that the best advice that I could give would be to avoid most of these people, because they seem to be rather frantic politicians of a sort. The other day, in the *Southern Review,* I think, I saw an article by Leo Spitzer, apparently an Austrian Jew, who is now at Johns Hopkins. It is a question whether such a man would have anything to say directly, but as a source he might be of interest. . . .

> About Rahv: he is a Jew and a Communist. For all that, he is
> a man of extraordinary intelligence. His position very definitely
> is that the poet must be the exponent of his time. Since that is
> something that Hegelians have in common with Marxists, he
> would be likely to do a brilliant job.
>
> Borgese was Professor of Aesthetics at Milan. Just why he is
> in this country I don't know; it may be that he is a Jew, an anti-
> Fascist. All I know is that at the present time he is teaching at
> the University of Chicago, and that what he has to say about
> what may be called the psychology of the poet seems to be
> worthwhile: very much so. (WSA)[7]

Finally, Stevens adds the name of Morton Zabel, whom he refers to as
"a Catholic," and then demurs: "in suggesting these . . . men I have not
paid any attention to their political or religious beliefs, if they have any"
(L 385).

What is noteworthy here is Stevens' ambivalence. He is evidently drawn
to intellectual brilliance (Spitzer, Rahv, Borgese) even as he instinctively
withdraws from what he condescendingly calls "these people." Again,
he is given to labels like "Jew," "Communist," "Catholic," "anti-Fas-
cist," even as he insists that he has no interest in political or religious
beliefs. He seems, in other words, to be obsessed by what he calls in
"The Noble Rider" "the pressure of reality," even as he abjures that
reality as alien to the purity of art. For isn't poetry (which is to say, in
Stevens' vocabulary, *lyric* poetry) supposed to avoid all rhetorical impurities? This is the impasse of lyric to which I shall later return.

By December 1941, at any rate, Stevens was beginning to plan his long
poem for the Cummington Press. In the correspondence, discussion of
the *Notes* now alternates with a new and consuming passion for genealogy. A week after Pearl Harbor, for example, Stevens writes to his sister
in Reading asking her to check up on a Mrs. Steinmetz, who had been
recommended as someone who might be able to tell him something about
the Zeller (maternal) side of his family. He also suggests to his sister that
she contact the Reading branch of the Sons of the Revolution for this
information. Perhaps this concern for familial origins was a way of escaping
from what Stevens was to call, in his prose note to *Parts of a World* (1942),
"the violent reality of war," in the presence of which "consciousness
takes the place of imagination."[8] Indeed, when Stevens does allude to the
war in the correspondence – and the instances are rare – he tends to play
the comedian. On February 7, 1942, for example, he tells Henry Church,
who had been suffering from angina, "Even if it should be true that your
heart occasionally calls attention in a most exciting way, think how the

Emperor of Japan and Hitler, who are said to have no hearts, feel every day of the year." (L 402). Not only is this in bad taste, it shows that Stevens can deal with actual men like Hitler and Hirohito only by putting them into some kind of fable: They must, it seems, take their places in the metaphoric country of the Arabian and Nanzia Nunzio.

This *pays de la métaphore* was not, however, to be divorced from a materiality of a different kind. On May 14, 1942, Stevens writes the letter cited earlier outlining the numerology of his *Notes toward a Supreme Fiction:* Thirty poems divided into three equal sections, each with a title. Further, thirty (poems) times seven (stanzas) times three (lines) equals 630 lines. One poem per page equals thirty pages, plus separate nearly blank pages for the subtitles: in short, a perfect geometric whole. Subsequent letters (May 19; June 1) express concern about the placement of line ends (Stevens disliked the look of runover lines or "tag ends"), and about the numbering system (Roman or arabic? numbers for the main divisions or not?). As for the physical appearance of the book, Stevens tells Katharine Frazier that he prefers "a light tan linen or buckram cover. If there are to be colored initials, then I very much prefer red and green to blue." And he suggests putting on the back of the jacket "a border consisting of a line or two of the poem beginning 'Soldier there is a war' [the epilogue], enough to state the idea" (L 408). (This plan was executed.) On June 5, the day after the Battle of Midway, Stevens adds, "I shall be greatly pleased to have the unbound copy [he had ordered one for himself] done on hand-made paper if you have it. I am expecting to have my copy bound by Gerhard Gerlach. He was a pupil of Wiemuller's at Leipsic [sic] and is working in New York at the present time. His bindings run into a lot of money, but, on the other hand, they are worth it." (WSA)

So it goes through the dark summer of 1942, when the Germans were pressing against the eastern front and the fighting in the Pacific was heavy. When *Notes* finally appeared in September in an edition of 273 copies, 190 were on Dutch Charchola paper, eighty on Worth Hand & Arrows, and three on Highclere, an English hand-made paper. Stevens' own copy was bound by Gerhard Gerlach in yellow oasis goat leather, the edge of the slipcase in matching leather. The design was made and executed in gold tooling on the binding; the title was designed and done with gouges (see L 420). Here was Stevens' tribute to his own Supreme Fiction, to the First Idea: "I am letting myself go on these bindings," he writes to Gerlach, "but after all, these are my own things and if I don't let myself go on them I don't know who will." (L 420)

No doubt the physical appearance of *Notes toward a Supreme Fiction* provided some comfort in a dark time. By September, when the book appeared, the war news was exacerbated by what Stevens evidently regarded as a personal disaster – his daughter Holly's decision, in her sophomore year, to leave Vassar. In "The Noble Rider" of 1941, Stevens had used the figure of Plato's charioteer in the *Phaedrus* as an emblem of the real, declaring, in a much-quoted statement, "The imagination loses vitality as it ceases to adhere to what is real" (NA 6). This and Stevens' related Paterian essays – or prose poems, as Harold Bloom rightly calls them[9] – are usually read as a defense of this doctrine, as a plea for "the interdependence of the imagination and reality as equals" (NA 27). But the longest portion of "The Noble Rider" is devoted to "the pressure of reality," a pressure that seems to make such "interdependence" all but impossible:

> The enormous influence of education is giving everyone a little learning, and in giving large groups considerably more . . . the expansion of the middle class with its common preference for realistic satisfactions; the penetration of the masses of people by the ideas of liberal thinkers . . . these are normal aspects of everyday life. The way we live and the way we work alike cast us out on reality. If fifty private houses were to be built in New York this year, it would be a phenomenon. We no longer live in homes but in housing projects and this is so whether the project is literally a project or a club, a dormitory, a camp or an apartment in River House. It is not only that there are more of us and that we are actually closer together. We are close together in every way. We lie in bed and listen to a broadcast from Cairo, and so on. There is no distance. We are intimate with people we have never seen and, unhappily, they are intimate with us. (NA 18)

Harold Bloom quite rightly, and a little uncomfortably, notes that Stevens' disparagement of apartment living finds its way into Canto II of "It Must be Abstract": "It is the celestial ennui of apartments / That sends us back to the first idea. . . ."[10] But Bloom, who regards the *Notes* as a strong misreading of Whitman, seems here to ignore the very real difference between the Stevens of "It Must be Abstract" and such Whitman catalogues as this one:

> The jour printer with gray head and gaunt jaws works at his
> case,
> He turns his quid of tobacco while his eyes blurr with the
> manuscript;
> The malform'd limbs are tied to the surgeon's table,

What is removed drops horrible in a pail;
The quadroon girl is sold at the auction-stand, the drunkard
    nods by the bar-room stove,
The machinist rolls up his sleeves, the policeman travels his
    beat, the gate-keeper marks who pass,
The young fellow drives the express-wagon, (I love him
    though I do not know him)[11]

For Stevens, such people are *other* and hence to be avoided. The workers'
revolution, he remarks in the essay, is merely "a revolution for more
pay" and hence trivial: "The time must be coming, when, as they leave
the factories, they will be passed through an air-chamber or a bar to
revive them for riot and reading." (NA 19) He then adds:

> I am sorry to have to add that to one that thinks, as Dr. [I. A.]
> Richards thinks, that poetry is the supreme use of language, some
> of the foreign universities in relation to our own appear to be, as
> far as the things of the imagination are concerned, as Verrocchio
> to the sculptor of the statue of General Jackson. (NA 19)

Poetry is the supreme use of language: here is adumbrated the famous
statement near the end of "The Noble Rider" that "[the poet] gives to
life the supreme fictions without which we are unable to conceive it"
(NA 31). But what we might call Stevens' Mallarméan drive toward
purification is accompanied by a peculiarly American – perhaps Henry
Jamesian – regard for Europe as the Great Good Place. For the "foreign
universities" Stevens mentions with such envy had been, by the spring
of 1941, virtually decimated, their faculties, Jewish and Christian alike,
taking refuge around the globe, especially in the United States – witness
the "Austrian Jew," Leo Spitzer, whom Stevens regards with such
ambivalence. But Stevens does not care to face such "news":

> For more than ten years now, there has been an extraordinary
> pressure of news . . . news, at first, of the collapse of our sys-
> tem, or, call it, of life; then of news of a new world . . . and
> finally news of a war, which was a renewal of what, if it was not
> the greatest war, became such by this continuation. And for more
> than ten years, the consciousness of the world has concentrated
> on events which have made the ordinary movement of life seem
> to be the movement of people in the intervals of a storm. (NA
> 20)

Such immersion in a "war-like whole," Stevens suggests, makes one
long for a time like the Napoleonic era, which "had little or no effect on

the poets and the novelists who lived in it. But Coleridge and Wordsworth and Sir Walter Scott and Jane Austen did not have to put up with
Napoleon and Marx and Europe." (NA 21)

These comments reveal Stevens to be rather less in tune with the early
Romantics than is commonly thought. "We are confronting," he declares
to the Princeton audience of 1941, "a set of events not only beyond our
power to reduce them and metamorphose them, but events that stir the
emotions to violence, that engage us in what is direct and immediate and
real" (NA 22). It is difficult to conceive of Wordsworth retreating from
engagement in this way – or Heine, or for that matter Whitman, for
whom "being intimate with people we have never seen" was precisely a
source of transcendence. No, Stevens (at least the Stevens of "The Noble
Rider") is less the Wordsworthian or Whitmanian poet than he is a belated
Symboliste. Indeed, the master text that stands behind *The Necessary Angel*
is Mallarmé's "Crise de vers" (1895), in which we read:

> One of the undeniable ideals of our time is to divide words into
> two different categories: first for vulgar or immediate, second,
> for essential purposes.
>   The first is for narrative, instruction or description. . . . The
> elementary use of language involves that universal *journalistic* style
> which characterizes all kinds of contemporary writing, with the
> exception of literature.

The language of poetry thus becomes wholly self-reflexive: "When I say:
'A flower!' then from the forgetfulness to which my voice consigns all
floral form, something different from the usual calyces arises, something
all music, essence, and softness: the flower which is absent from all bou-
quets."[12] Or, as Stevens was to put it in a 1948 poem called "The Bouquet," "a growth / of the reality of the eye, an artifice . . . a flitter that
reflects itself" (CP 448).

In the related chronicle called "Le Livre, instrument spirituel," Mallarmé sets up a dichotomy between "the Newspaper" and "the Book."
The newspaper is "large-sized" and "open," whereas the "foldings" of
the book have "an almost religious significance." The newspaper inflicts
on us "the monotonousness of its eternally unbearable columns"; the
"fragile and inviolable book," on the other hand, "is perfect Music, and
cannot be anything else." The Book, as Mallarmé defines it, is both sacred
rite and, metaphorically, the moment of passionate discharge. The
Newspaper knows no such moments: "with its endless line of posters
and proof sheets it makes for improvisation."[13]

Improvisation, once an integral part of the poetic enterprise – think of
Byron's *Don Juan* or Heine's *Germany: A Winter's Tale* – is here ruled out

of court. Such polarization of art and improvisation, poetic and non-poetic language, the Book and the Newspaper, surely has political overtones. As Michel Beaujour suggests in a recent essay on the prose poem:

> . . . an absolute distinction between journalistic cacography and artful writing is purely ideological and does not stand up to linguistic or rhetorical scrutiny: it is all a question of taste, and should ideology so decree, *bad* taste might become axiological king of the castle. We know this upset did indeed take place with futurism, Dadaism, surrealism, and their sequels: posters and newspapers became paradigms of artfulness.[14]

This is an important point. I have discussed elsewhere[15] the rupture in the lyric paradigm made by the Russian and Italian Futurists, as well as by American poets like Pound – whose *Cantos* represent what Michael Bernstein has called "a decisive turning point in modern poetics" in that they "open for verse the capacity to include domains of experience [the historical document, the personal letter, the shopping list] long since considered alien territory."[16] For Stevens, however, poetry always remains *lyric* poetry, as late Romantic theory (if not always the poetry) had defined it – the poem as short verse utterance (or sequence of such utterances) in which a single speaker expresses, in figurative language, his subjective vision of truth, a truth culminating in a unique insight or epiphany that unites poet and reader. Stevens is concerned with the "essential poem at the centre of things," "the instant of speech" (CP 440). In "The Figure of the Youth as Virile Poet" (1943), he says, "There can be no poetry without the personality of the poet" (NA 46), and again, "There is a life apart from politics. It is this life that the youth as virile poet lives, in a kind of radiant and productive atmosphere." (NA 57) And he quotes Mallarmé's "Le Vierge, le vivace, et le bel aujourd'hui."

Such a poetics, belated as it was in Stevens' time, could and did produce exquisite lyrics of subjectivity (and, according to Harold Bloom, subjectivity has been "ever since Wordsworth's Copernican revolution"[17] the poet's only subject). Stevens is at his most assured, I would argue, when he makes no gesture toward the world of "prose reality" – the world of "what is direct and immediate and real," which he finds so distasteful – but rather explores, like his own "Rabbit as King of the Ghosts," the ways of becoming "A self that touches all edges" (CP 209). "Thirteen Ways of Looking at a Blackbird" provides one example; another, from the period of *Notes,* is "No Possum, No Sop, No Taters," which begins with these abrupt couplets:

> He is not here, the old sun,
> As absent as if we were asleep.

> The field is frozen. The leaves are dry.
> Bad is final in this light.   (CP 293)

Here image and syntax mime the movement of consciousness; Stevens works with the most minimal stage properties, bringing us gradually around to the turn, a very slight turn:

> The crow looks rusty as he rises up.
> Bright is the malice of his eye . . .
>
> One joins him there for company.
> But at a distance, in another tree.   (CP 294)

It is possible to transcend the bleak air and broken limbs of January ("it must be possible"), but one cannot expect too much; the crow's world can never, after all, be one's own. But here at least there is the "distance" whose absence Stevens deplores when, in The Noble Rider and the Sound of Words, he talks about his fellow men and women. In a world of "stalks . . . firmly rooted in ice," one must have a mind of winter: the placement of the observer "in another tree" has its own eccentric design.

Notes toward a Supreme Fiction adopts a rather different stance toward the problem of lyric. In an unusually candid letter to Hi Simons (January 1940), Stevens writes:

> People say that I live in a world of my own: that sort of thing. Instead of seeking therefore for a "relentless contact," I have been interested in what might be described as an attempt to achieve the normal, the central. So stated, this puts the thing out of all proportion, in respect to its relation to the context of life. Of course, I don't agree with the people who say that I live in a world of my own; I think that I am perfectly normal, but I see that there is a center. For instance, a photograph of a lot of fat men and women in the woods, drinking beer and singing Hi-li Hi-lo convinces me that there is a normal that I ought to try to achieve. (L 352)

Of course Stevens doesn't really want to bring a lot of fat men and women drinking beer into his lyric discourse. His solution is to let them exist in the title of a given poem ("A Lot of People Bathing in a Stream," for example), or to turn to narrative. In the case of *Notes,* he invents a series of fables – whimsical little allegorical tales in which characters like "the maiden Bawda" and "the Canon Aspirin" and "the planter" illustrate different facets of the poet's longing for the Supreme Fiction, along with his gradually growing recognition of its existence only in the "fluent mundo" of poetic language, a series of endless figural repetitions.

Helen Vendler has observed that, although the characters in *Notes* are indeed allegorical figures, "they represent the tangible rather than the desired," that which is "quotidian, recognizable, accessible, or at least naturalized" (OEW 169). But "quotidian" and "recognizable" in what sense? How, for example, are such fables as those of MacCullough and the Major Man (Cantos VIII–X of "It Must be Abstract") related to the explicit political poem, "Soldier, there is a war," the epilogue to *Notes toward a Supreme Fiction?* I wish to take up these questions by positing the possibility of giving a political rather than the usual straightforward literary (which is to say, figural and structural) reading of the Major Man cantos.

Canto VII of "It Must be Abstract" opens with the lines, "It feels good as it is without the giant, / A thinker of the first idea"; and the opening of Canto VIII is obviously an elaboration of this concept:

> Can we compose a castle-fortress-home,
> Even with the help of Viollet-le-Duc,
> And set the MacCullough there as major man?
>
> The first idea is an imagined thing.
> The pensive giant prone in violet space
> May be the MacCullough, an expedient,
>
> Logos and logic, crystal hypothesis.   (CP 387)

The major commentaries on the *Notes* – those of Roy H. Pearce, Frank Kermode, Helen Vendler, Frank Doggett, Harold Bloom, Joseph Riddel[18] – are in surprising agreement about the meanings propounded by this difficult lyric. Indeed, despite seeming differences, the premises that govern the various interpretations of a given Stevens poem have remained remarkably constant. To illustrate this point, I want to look at two exegeses, made fifteen years apart, by Harold Bloom, and then compare these to two others, again fifteen years apart, by a critic who takes a seemingly antithetical theoretical position, Joseph Riddel. (I shall be speaking of Bloom I and II, Riddel I and II.)

Here is Bloom I (1963) on *Notes:*

> Stevens had the radiant fortune that attends only the great poets: his most ambitious poem is his best. The six-hundred and fifty-nine lines of *Notes toward a Supreme Fiction* constitute his central attempt to relieve the imaginative poverty of his time, and they establish him as I think the central poet of that time, bringing to us the consolations of a poetic humanism as Wordsworth brought them to his contemporaries. (TCV 76)

In what sense can the "consolations of a poetic humanism" (note the Arnoldian cast of the phrase) really atone for what was happening to the mass of human beings in this time, not only the "imaginative poverty" but the death and terror? Bloom does not raise this issue. He begins by noting that the title, "It Must be Abstract," refers to the poet's need "to abstract or withdraw himself from outworn conceptualizations of reality and to live in the world, yet outside the existing conceptions of it . . . by fabricating his fictions" (TCV 77). So, in Canto VIII, which presents us with the poet "in the vitality of his ironic extravagance," we proceed from the "crystal hypothesis" of the MacCullough "who remains merely MacCullough, to the major man who evades our tautologies" (TCV 81). There are two means by which "That imagined thing, the first idea, moves in on the MacCullough." The first is a vision of MacCullough as the "figure of the youth as virile poet, the 'beau linguist' conceived as a young god" (see the last four tercets of Canto VIII). "From this chant of a possible incarnation," writes Bloom, "Stevens descends to deliberate the advent of a more probable version of the major man. We must put aside the idiom of apotheosis, 'the romantic intoning, the declaimed clairvoyance' [Canto IX, line 1] and be content plainly to propound a coming of the major man more subtly modest in its manner" (TCV 82). Not major man as a young god, then, but "as an old tramp, the comedian 'in his old coat, / His slouching pantaloons, beyond the town, / Looking for what was, where it used to be'." Bloom goes on to quote the final tercet:

> It is of him, ephebe, to make, to confect
> The final elegance, not to console
> Nor sanctify, but plainly to propound.   (CP 389)

He concludes:

> The ultimate elegance is the imagined land, to be fabricated by the ephebe out of this battered hero who is beyond loss. The whole burden of *Notes* rests upon these closing lines and their admonition. . . . our idea of man is a final belief in a last-ditch sense of finality; major man is abler in the "abstract than in his singular," a figure of capable imagination only when withdrawn from his not very fecund world. Confronted by this "inanimate, difficult visage," we know as ephebes that our hard obligation is "plainly to propound" what we have abstracted, to present without ornament, the naked poem, the vulnerable confrontation. (p. 83)[19]

It is this admonition that leads, by the circuitous path of "It Must Change," to the final cantos of "It Must Give Pleasure," where the poet learns "not to impose" an order "but to discover." In the final "heroic integration" when the poet is at one with himself, "what is outside the self can be dismissed without fear of solipsistic self-absorption, for the self has joined major man" (TCV 94).

Bloom's 1977 reading is somewhat more skeptical of the poem's "heroic integration[s]"; indeed, he declares that he is "no longer particularly happy" with his earlier analysis (POC 168). For one thing, in the interim Stevens' letters had been published, and in Bloom's words "the fable of MacCullough [is] glossed by Stevens with considerable unease of spirit" (POC 189). The relevant letter is to Hi Simons (January 12, 1943):

> MacCullough is MacCullough; MacCullough is any name, any man. The trouble with humanism is that man as God remains man, but there is an extension of man, the leaner being, in fiction, a possibly more than human human, a composite human. The act of recognizing him is the act of this leaner being moving in on us. (L 434)

Most commentators have taken Stevens at his word: "MacCullough is any name, any man," and an idealized humanism that wants to turn such a man into a god must be qualified by what Stevens calls in Canto VIII "the leaner being." But MacCullough, as Bloom rightly notes, is not just any old name: "MacCullough was the name of a hardheaded clan, producing eminent political economists, geologists, and even the American Secretary of the Treasury when Stevens was a student at Harvard. . . . we expect Whitman and not MacCullough to be experiencing poetic incarnation while lounging by the sea" (POC 189). To transform this emblem of stubborn and intransigent reality is thus not easy:

> Unlike Viollet-le-Duc, Stevens is not interested in that kind of restoration in which you put false fronts on edifices. . . . In the MacCullough we confront Whitman assimilated to Nietzsche . . . an American Over-Man, a grand trope or noble synecdoche of Power, power that compounds the ocean as universe of death, and language. . . . Canto IX both heralds the full-grown poet as major man and makes it impossible to describe him or recognize him if ever he comes. . . . We cannot see him, we cannot think him, we cannot name him, and yet "he is, he is, / This foundling of the infected past." The Emersonian, apocalyptic dismissal of history could go no further. (POC 189–190)

Given this dismissal of history, of which I shall have more to say, the poet's admonition, at the end of Canto X, "not to console / Nor sanctify but plainly to propound" is now interpreted more aggressively as meaning that "it is our burden to put our own version of major man forward for consideration." It looks ahead to the "great Canto VIII" of "It Must Give Pleasure," with its central question, "What am I to believe?" – a question, Bloom now declares categorically, that "impl[ies] the single answer 'I am to believe in a fiction of the self, in a trope of myself'.' (POC 212) In the privileged moment of Canto VIII, says Bloom, "we are *in* the world of the pleasure principle, the world of the supreme fiction or of the solitary self as mortal god" (POC 215). That this is an evasion of "truth" does not matter "because the truth either is or becomes death. The ultimate trope of *pathos* is 'the fiction that results from feeling,' a lie against time, or rather against time's unflickering 'It was'." (POC 217)

Now let us to see to what extent Riddel's readings of the *Notes* qualify Bloom's analyses. Here is Riddel I, in 1965 still a thorough and conscientious explicator, on the MacCullough:

> As first idea, the "pensive giant" is also the "crystal hypothesis,' man become "Logos," a humanistic extension of finite man into creator of the infinite idea. As a "Beau linguist," he is both poet and poet's creation. Major man, in brief, extends Stevens' search for the man-hero to replace the divine-hero. . . .
>
> [The] image of the MacCullough as man imagining (a dramatic realization of Emerson's "Man Thinking" or Whitman lying on Paumanok's shores) symbolizes the proper intercourse, man become his world as the world becomes his. . . . Canto 8, in sum, is a reworking of the hero myth, man taking on the dress of his world . . . and in that attire proving himself to be "Logos and logic" of the place where he resides. . . .
>
> [Major man] is not a form so much as a sense of human possibility. . . . He is neither transcendent deity nor anthropomorphic symbol, but a transparence of the ephebe, the humanistic myth made in man's cosmic image. . . . The poet's responsibility to "confect" this figure turns away from the god without, acknowledges the self within. (CE 173–74)

Note that Riddel's focus, like Bloom's, is on the Emersonian and Whitmanian lineage of the MacCullough, and that his account of the influx of the "leaner being," transforming the MacCullough into a humanistic myth, is also very similar to Bloom's. Like Bloom, Riddel suggests that the Major Man cantos look ahead to the conclusion of "It Must Give Pleasure," where the "self within," as Bloom has also posited, becomes the image "of a world of which man is master, the man-hero who comes to accept what is humanly possible and desire no more. The ephebe becomes a poet, lover of the 'Fat girl,' the vital heart of the world, the procreative source. . . . Man possessing the world in tropes possesses finally and irreducibly himself." (CE 182–83) This is the epiphany of the final tercet:

> Until flicked by feeling, in a gildered street,
> I call you by name, my green, my fluent mundo.
> You will have stopped revolving except in crystal.

"Except in poetry," Riddel explains, "in the self whose names master but do not deny the fluent mundo" (CE 183).

Between this reading and Riddel's second (1980) falls the shadow of Derrida. *Notes,* like every other text, is now to be deconstructed, and it should immediately be said that Stevens lends himself especially well to such procedures. The "supreme fiction" is now viewed as "the closure of totalization . . . that poetry repeatedly reinvents and yet precludes in the 'war' of its incessant, revolutionary writing" (D&B 316). *Notes* is now seen as "the great text of this writing against the 'book' . . . it is a master text that masters nothing" (D&B 316). For "to think the 'first idea' or the name of the origin of the system, one has first to think or be thought by that system" (D&B 318).

"If *Notes* has an *argument,*" says Riddel, now calling his own earlier analysis into question, "it occurs as a movement of negations, a dismantling and reworking of the venerable triad of metaphysico/poetics, the dialectics of subject/object that is mediated and regulated by the illusion of resemblance." How does such "dismantling" work?

> "It Must be Abstract" revolves the structure of every idealism
> and the dream of proper negation. If poetic reflection must think
> away the "giant" or "thinker of the first idea," revealing that the
> "academies" are "like structures in a mist" (CP, p. 386), it can-
> not think away the functional necessity of the subject. So the
> "major man," reduced to "expedient" and "crystal hypothesis,"
> must replace the "giant" and this suggests a restoration of the
> very system that has been negated or reversed. Poem VIII of part
> one underlines the artifice, the machinery, of the restoration.
> (D&B 321)

Riddel goes on to quote the first three lines of the canto. Ignoring what is surely an ironic allusion to Viollet-le-Duc, he continues to insist upon his Derridean paradigm:

Like a Viollet-le-Duc restoration, the new structure will be more
original than its predecessor. It is marked through and through
as a fiction, a "machine" of "Swiss perfection," for it reveals
that the thinker of the first idea has always been a figure labori-
ously reconstructed and installed within a system where it stands
for the origin of the system. "Major man" as the "exponent" of
the "idea of man" is clearly a propounded or invented figure,
the abstraction (the clown of poem x), substituted for the sanc-
tified giant or the transcendental fiction of the thinker/author/god.
The poet is always de-centered . . . suffering from the "celestial
ennui of apartments." . . . But he dreams recurrently of restoring word to thing, of achieving a natural language . . . even if
in a fiction he knows not to be true. (D&B 321–22)

This last sentence brings us up short: The poet, we are told, suffers from
the "celestial ennui of apartments" but "dreams recurrently of restoring
word to thing," even if in a fiction he knows to be false. Despite the
Derridean terminology, Riddel finally has the poem say precisely what
Stevens himself repeatedly said: "The final belief is to believe in a fiction
which you know to be a fiction, there being nothing else." (OP 163).
Indeed, Riddel's Deconstructionist reading merely turns Bloom's reading (or Pearce's, or Doggett's, or Kermode's) another half circle: whereas
all seem to agree that "major man" is a necessary invention, an elaborate
"confection" which makes it possible for the poet to acknowledge "the
self within," Riddel argues that this making of fictions is itself a fiction,
"unveiling the ground of that fiction in the 'aberration' of metaphor."
"The poem," he says, "reveals the 'muddy centre' of our origins . . . to
be not a 'truth' that has expelled us . . . but a 'fluent mundo' of poetic
language, the 'Theatre / Of Trope'." But for Bloom, this "Theatre / Of
Trope" is also central: "The truth either is or becomes death," and "the
ultimate trope of *pathos* is 'the fiction that results from feeling'." (POC
217) Reading Riddel against Bloom, one thus has the curious feeling
that, as Stevens puts it in the *Notes,* the "man-hero" (in this case evidently the critic) "is not the exceptional monster, / But he that of repetition is most master" (CP 406).

What does this mastery of (critical) repetitions tell us? Perhaps that we
will continue to perform similar readings on texts like *Notes toward a
Supreme Fiction* unless we are willing to ask not just *how* meanings are
created in the poem but *why*. That is to say, not *how* the "heroic integration" in which "the self has joined major man" takes place – a process
Bloom describes masterfully – but *why* one would want such a thing to
happen. "The poet is always de-centered," says Riddel, ". . . but he dreams

recurrently of restoring word to thing." Stevens' poet, perhaps – but does every poet so dream, and why? Again, why should a poem posit the notion of a "figural space" where "supreme fictions" are written, and what does it mean to invent such a fiction-to-be-dismantled? Does Duchamp invent such supreme fictions, or Beckett? Does Pope's poetry create such "figural spaces" – or Swift's?

Let us look once more at the opening of Canto VIII (Part One), this time as a statement, however evasive and coded, of a particular ideology:

> Can we compose a castle-fortress-home,
> Even with the help of Viollet-le Duc,
> And set the MacCullough there as major man?

Here three questions immediately come to mind: (1) What does it signify, in the middle of World War II – when the real Major Men included such names as Hitler, Mussolini, and Stalin – to posit the desirability, however fleeting, of Major Man? It is true, of course, as Bloom says, that the poem urges us to "put aside the idiom of apotheosis . . . and be content plainly to propound a coming of major man more subtly modest in its manner" (TCV 82). But this begs the question of why one should want such a coming in the first place. (2) Why is the candidate for Major Manhood called MacCullough? (3) Why, in the MacCullough fable, as in the stories of Nanzia Nunzio or the captain and the maiden Bawda, does Stevens "confect" allegorical figures – shadow puppets, really – rather than referring to real people as does, say, Yeats or Pound?

Let us begin with the second question. Despite Stevens' disclaimer that "MacCullough is any name, any man," the name MacCullough obviously carries particular overtones (whether or not Stevens had a certain secretary of the treasury by that name in mind). MacCullough is, of course, a good Wasp name; it is not, assuredly, Spitzer or Rahv or Borgese. Again, MacCullough connotes racial purity; unlike, say, MacSweeney, which is Scotch-Irish, it is not contaminated. Third, *the* MacCullough connotes masculinity, a strong "hard-headed clan," as Bloom puts it, with a tradition of prowess in combat – the very opposite, surely, of the feminine, the weaker vessel. Indeed, given the context of European fascism, the very naming of "the MacCullough" brings to mind the stereotype of Aryan purity, the master race. If, then, "MacCullough himself lay lounging by the sea, / Drowned in its washes, reading in the sound, / About the thinker of the first idea," would he, as Stevens hopes he might, "take habit, whether from wave or phrase, / Or power of the wave, or deepened speech, / Or a leaner being, moving in on him, / Of greater aptitude and apprehension"? These lines suggest that the poet does not regard the MacCullough with indifference. There is a certain attraction to the type

– on November 21, 1935, Stevens writes to Ronald Lane Latimer, "that Mussolini is right, practically, has certainly a great deal to be said for it" (L 295) – even though he knows that the MacCullough must undergo a real transformation, "a leaner being moving in on him." But because it is difficult to imagine how the MacCulloughs of the world are, in fact, to be changed, Stevens finally replaces him with another "crystal hypothesis" – that of the little man in the "old coat, those sagging pantaloons." And in the course of the poem, even this "miserable" "chieftain" will be left behind, as the poet's vision turns increasingly inward.

Notes toward a Supreme Fiction, we are told, works toward a dismantling of such terms as "First Idea," "Major Man," "gold centre," and "amassing harmony." In the end, the poet comes around to the understanding that there are only

> the vast repetitions final in
> Themselves and, therefore, good, the going round
>
> And round and round, the merely going round,
> Until merely going round is a final good,
> The way wine comes at a table in a wood.
>
> And we enjoy like men, the way a leaf
> Above the table spins its constant spin,
> So that we look at it with pleasure, look
>
> At it spinning its eccentric measure.   (CP 405–406)

How do the "vast repetitions" square with "the final good"? It seems that the poet, far from immersing himself in the flux, the "merely going round," is still reaching out for the First Idea, the Supreme Fiction. Not knowing quite how to assimilate what he calls, in his letter to Hi Simons, the "normal" of "a lot of fat men and women in the woods, drinking beer and singing Hi-li Hi-lo," Stevens (whose own drink "at a table in a wood" is wine) produces the "Fat girl, terrestrial, my summer, my night," the green queen of his "fluent mundo," who, "flicked by feeling, in a gildered street," will have "stopped revolving except in crystal." One thinks of the Steuben glass in the windows of Fifth Avenue, the crystal globe containing the figures inside it – arrested motion, a beautiful stasis. Not surprisingly, this final canto modulates into the epilogue about the Soldier, an epilogue that even Stevens' most fervent admirers have found problematic.[20] This poem, lines from which were used for the border on the book jacket of the Cummington Press edition, poses an equation between Poet and Soldier: the "poet's war," we are told, "depends on yours [the soldier's]. The two are one." But whereas the soldier's "war ends. And after it you return / With six meats and twelve wines or else without / To walk another room," the poet's war with language is one that "never ends." And hence, "The soldier is poor without the poet's lines."

Note that it would have been impossible to make these statements in the concrete, with reference to the poet's own person (I, Wallace Stevens) or to a particular soldier (Private First Class Jonathan Smithfield), much less to an actual war hero like Colin Kelly. The poem's cast of characters "Must Be Abstract" – the Soldier, the Fat Girl, the President, the Major Man, and finally the Poet.

Now let us return to the question of genre. In discussing the lyric poem, Mikhail Bakhtin says:

> In genres that are poetic in the narrow sense, the natural dialogization of the word is not put to artistic use, the word is sufficient unto itself and does not presume alien utterances beyond its own boundaries. Poetic style is by convention suspended from any mutual interaction with alien discourse, any allusion to alien discourse.[21]

Bakhtin, writing in the thirties, was distinguishing the lyric from the novel; but today we can apply this distinction to poetry itself, to the difference between what we might call "straight lyric" (Dickinson, Crane, Frost, Stevens) and the "impure" collage poetry of the Pound tradition.[22] With regard to the former, Bakhtin makes an important point:

> . . . the language of poetic genres, when they approach their stylistic limit, often becomes authoritarian, dogmatic and conservative, sealing itself off from the influence of extraliterary social dialects. Therefore such ideas as a special "poetic language," a "language of the gods," a "priestly language of poetry" and so forth could flourish on poetic soil. It is noteworthy that the poet, should he not accept the given literary language, will sooner resort to the artificial creation of a new language specifically for poetry than he will to the exploitation of actual available social dialects. (p. 287)

This perfectly characterizes what I see as the problematic of *Notes toward a Supreme Fiction*. It is a lyric sequence that makes repeated gestures toward what Stevens would call "the normal" of "actual available social dialects," towards the Chaplinesque figure in the sagging pantaloons; but the poet's deep-seated suspicion of the "impurities of everyday life"—in Bakhtin's terms, of the alien utterances beyond the boundaries of the self-sufficient world – can find an outlet only in the extravagant metaphoricity that is Stevens' signature, particularly in the earlier poetry.

Joseph Riddel and others refer frequently to the "openness" and "incompleteness" of the *Notes,* the "deferred finality" that characterizes its "writing against the 'book'." My own sense is that this is wishful thinking. Like Bloom's, Riddel's own interpretation suggests that, even discounting the epilogue, the poem moves inexorably toward its "crystal hypothesis" in the last cantos, to the sense that "Yes, that. / They will get it straight one day at the Sorbonne" – a sentence that naturally delights the Deconstructionists but does not, in fact, dismantle what Bakhtin would call the poem's monologic discourse. Even the geometric perfection of the Cummington Press book (one poem per page, ten poems per section, seven tercets per poem, the three group titles on separate pages) reflects Stevens' need to have his "fluent mundo" revolve *in crystal.*

Interestingly enough, Stevens himself seems to have sensed the limitations of his "Theatre / Of Trope" more fully than have his ephebes. As he put it in a poem written two years before the *Notes,* "Of Modern Poetry":

> then the theatre was changed
> To something else. Its past was a souvenir.
> It has to be living, to learn the speech of the place.
> It has to face the men of the time and to meet
> The women of the time. It has to think about war
> And it has to find what will suffice.   (CP 240)

But if these things were to be accomplished, there would no longer be the need for a Major Man, not even as a "crystal hypothesis" to be dismantled. And the Supreme Fiction would then be that we should ever deem such a fiction to be necessary. Indeed, the "confecting" of Supreme Fictions belongs to our history – a history Stevens longed to erase even as it now haunts our own reception of his poetry.

NOTES

1 Unpublished letter in the Wallace Stevens Archive, Huntington Library, San Marino. Material from the Wallace Stevens Archive is subsequently cited as WSA.

2 *Letters of Wallace Stevens,* ed. Holly Stevens (New York: Knopf, 1966), p. 397. Subsequently cited in text as L.

3 Frank Kermode, *"Notes toward a Supreme Fiction:* A Commentary," Annali Dell' Institute Universitario Orientale (Naples: 1961); Kermode, *Wallace Stevens* (Edinburgh and London: Oliver and Boyd, 1967), pp. 111–19; Helen Vendler, *On Extended Wings: Wallace Stevens' Longer Poems* (Cambridge: Harvard University Press, 1969), pp. 168–205, subsequently cited as OEW;

Harold Bloom, *"Notes Toward a Supreme Fiction:* A Commentary," in *Wallace Stevens: A Collection of Critical Essays,* ed. Marie Boroff (Englewood Cliffs, N.J.: Prentice-Hall, 1963), pp. 76–95, subsequently cited as TCV; Bloom, *Wallace Stevens: The Poems of Our Climate* (Ithaca and London: Cornell University Press, 1977), pp. 167–218, subsequently cited as POC; Joseph N. Riddel, *The Clairvoyant Eye: The Poetry and Poetics of Wallace Stevens* (Baton Rouge: Louisiana State University Press, 1965), pp. 165–85, subsequently cited as CE; Riddel, "Metaphoric Staging: Stevens' Beginning Again of the 'End of the Book'," in *Wallace Stevens: A Celebration,* ed. Frank Doggett and Robert Buttell (Princeton: Princeton University Press, 1980), pp. 308–38, subsequently cited as D&B.

4   "Adagia," in *Opus Posthumous,* ed. Samuel French Morse (New York: Knopf, 1957), p. 179. Subsequently cited as OP.

5   Cf. the testimonies about Church collected in Peter Brazeau's oral biography, *Parts of A World: Wallace Stevens Remembered* (New York: Random House, 1983). Frederick Morgan, for example, remembers meeting Church at Princeton in 1942: "He was a terribly nice man and certainly a very intelligent one, but lacking in energy. I remember him saying to Tate one day that he had read two or three pages of some book of poetry by one of the well-thought-of poets of the day and that he'd gotten so tired he had to lie down and take a nap." (p. 219) See also pp. 217–30 for various accounts of Barbara Church's cocktail parties in New York in the fifties.

6   "The Noble Rider and the Sound of Words" was first published by Allen Tate in *The Language of Poetry* (Princeton, 1942), together with essays by Philip Wheelwright, Cleanth Brooks, and I. A. Richards. It then appeared in 1951 in *The Necessary Angel: Essays on Reality and the Imagination* (New York: Vintage Books, 1967), pp. 1–36. Subsequently cited as NA.

7   In *L* (p. 384) the words "he is a Jew and a Communist. For all that" have been excised, so that the sentence reads, "About Rahv [. . .] he is a man of extraordinary intelligence."

8   See Wallace Stevens, *The Palm at the End of the Mind: Selected Poems and a Play* (New York: Knopf, 1971), p. 206.

9   See Bloom, *Poems of our Climate,* p. 179.

10   Wallace Stevens, *Collected Poems of Wallace Stevens* (1954; New York: Knopf, 1961), p. 381. Subsequently cited as CP.

11   Walt Whitman, "Song of Myself," in *Leaves of Grass,* ed. Sculley Bradley and Harold W. Blodgett (New York: Norton, 1973), p. 42.

12   Stéphane Mallarmé, "Crisis in Poetry," trans. Bradford Cook, in Richard Ellmann and Charles Feidelson, eds., *The Modern Tradition: Backgrounds of Modern Literature* (New York: Oxford, 1965), pp. 110–12. For the original, see "Crise de vers," *Oeuvres complètes,* ed. Henri Mondor and G. Jean-Aubrey (Paris: Éditions Gallimard, Bibliothèque de la Pléiade, 1945), pp. 366–68.

13   Stéphane Mallarmé, "The Book: A Spiritual Instrument," trans. Bradford Cook, in Stéphane Mallarmé, *Selected Poetry and Prose* (New York: New Directions, 1982), pp. 80–84; cf. *Oeuvres complètes,* pp. 378–82.

14   Michel Beaujour, "Short Epiphanies: Two Contextual Approaches to the

French Prose Poem," in *The Prose Poem in France: Theory and Practice,* ed. Mary Ann Caws and Hermine Riffaterre (New York: Columbia University Press, 1983), pp. 55–56.

15   See "The Invention of Collage," in *Collage,* ed. Jeanine Parisier Plottel (New York: New York Literary Forum, 1983), pp. 5–47.

16   Michael André Bernstein, *The Tale of the Tribe: Ezra Pound and the Modern Verse Epic* (Princeton: Princeton University Press, 1980), p. 40.

17   Harold Bloom, "The Internalization of Quest Romance" (1968), in *The Ringers in the Tower: Studies in Romantic Tradition* (Chicago: University of Chicago Press, 1971), pp. 18–19.

18   Roy Harvey Pearce, *The Continuity of American Poetry* (Princeton: Princeton University Press, 1965), pp. 393–400; Frank Doggett, "This Invented World: Stevens' 'Notes toward a Supreme Fiction'," in *The Act of the Mind: Essays on the Poetry of Wallace Stevens,* ed. Roy Harvey Pearce and J. Hillis Miller (Baltimore: The Johns Hopkins Press, 1965), pp. 13–28. The others are listed in note 3. Bloom's two studies are subsequently cited as TCV and POC; Riddel's as CE and D&B.

19   In *Wallace Stevens: The Making of a Poem* (Baltimore and London: The Johns Hopkins Press, 1980), Frank Doggett makes some interesting refinements on this point: "The MacCullough is what he is, a fictive person to stand for the idea of man elevated by humanism to take the place of deity. This is the reason for showing the MacCullough in the sky. . . . In the second schema, Stevens places the MacCullough by the sea – 'drowned in its washes' – to indicate how this imagined figure might be modified by immersion in the reality of the world. . . . what the poem [Canto VIII] says [is]: if an idealized conception of man, like that of humanism, is modified by a more realistic version (the leaner being) . . . then that conception will be more in accord with the natural world and more capable of the arts of man." See pp. 99–101. Cf. Kermode, *"Notes toward a Supreme Fiction:* A Commentary," p. 183; Pearce, *Continuity of American Poetry,* pp. 396–97.

20   In *On Extended Wings,* Helen Vendler observes: "After the fine fluidities of the last canto, the epilogue to *Notes* is something of an anticlimax, repeating earlier material and resting on the rather too simply put interdependence of the man of action and the man of words." (p. 205) Cf. Bloom, *The Poems of Our Climate,* p. 216.

21   Mikhail Bakhtin, "Discourse in the Novel" (1934–35), in *The Dialogic Imagination: Four Essays,* ed. Michael Holquist (Austin and London: University of Texas Press, 1981), pp. 285–87. This whole essay, with its discussion of monologic versus dialogic discourse, is most helpful in considering Stevens' view of poetry.

22   See my forthcoming *The Dance of the Intellect: Studies in the Pound Tradition* (Cambridge University Press).

4

Effects of an Analogy:
Wallace Stevens and Painting

BONNIE COSTELLO

Writers have habitually directed their nostalgia for presence onto the visual arts. While painting is a kind of language, its sensuous immediacy helps it to overcome the distance inherent in representation in a way that the arbitrary signing of words cannot. Stevens frequently compared the enterprise of painting with his own of poetry, and often expressed a yearning for the condition of the visual arts. The many references Stevens makes to painting and to artists in poems, prose, and correspondence demonstrate the central place it held in his reflective life. "On my death there will be found carved on my heart . . . the name of Aix-en-Provence," he wrote in a letter to Thomas McGreevy.[1] It is significant that we should find the name, not the image of Cézanne's home carved there. For Stevens expressed his admiration for the visual arts not in imitation, but rather in allusion.

Michel Benamou surveyed the intricate subject of Stevens and painting in his 1959 study, "Poetry and Painting," and offered some valuable direction for appreciating Stevens' pictorial qualities and conceptual affinities to the visual arts.[2] But we need a more precise view of what may have attracted Stevens to the visual arts and what poetic use he made of his experience of painting.

One can say clearly what approaches Stevens did not take. He seldom used painting as a focusing device (as did Auden), a formal model (as did Williams), an image of the still moment (as did Keats and Eliot), or a source of emblemata (as Moore so often did). Stevens' poems do not, for the most part, visualize their subjects, making the reader a beholder of an imagined pictorial space. In fact, Stevens' poetry hardly resembles painting at all. He did not need to copy the effects of painting because he had available to him a whole array of *literary* devices and effects by which absent qualities are imported into a work. It is a mistake, I think, to match Stevens to this or that movement in painting, to this or that artist, for he suggests the entire enterprise of painting through naming, allusion, metaphor, narration, argument, and other literary means. Hals, Poussin, Claude, Constable, Corot, Dufy, Picasso are invoked, not imitated. The elements and techniques of painting – light, color, shape, line, plane, space, grisaille, chiaroscuro, etching – are not approximated in language but brought to mind. Stevens does not abandon poetic genres for painterly ones – portrait, still life, landscape – but borrows their associations. These subtle differences distinguish Stevens from other moderns – Williams, Stein, Apollinaire – who responded to other possibilities in the visual arts.

Williams, for instance, thought of words as "pigments put on." In an interview with Walter Sutton he remarked: "I've attempted to fuse the poetry and the painting, to make it the same thing."[3] Several books have been dedicated to exploring what Williams meant by this and similar comments. Bram Djikstra's ground-breaking study, *Hieroglyphics of a New Speech,* studied Williams' attraction to the special kinds of seeing claimed by Modernist art: analytic cubism and its methods of fragmentation and multiple perspective; the assemblages of collage; the isolation and intensification of objects by American painters like Charles Demuth and Marsden Hartley. Most recently, Henry Sayre's *The Visual Text of William Carlos Williams* argues that Williams' response to painting is based on form rather than image, and examines the tension between the experience of the page and of visual rhyme and representational and aural structures.[4]

All the studies of Williams agree that he takes the analogy with painting literally and strives for an equivalency of effect in words. Stevens' relation to painting is a far more figurative and conceptual one. He is less interested in the practice of painting than in its theory, quoting Picasso's notion of art as a "horde of destructions" and Klee's notion of "the organic center of all movement in time and place."[5] He was less interested in the particulars of technique (the building up of surface against illusion in Cézanne, or the breaking and reassembling in Gris) than in the condition of visual art and the special experience of beauty suggested within that condition (Cézanne's struggle for realization, or Gris' freeing of the imagination from the tyranny of the eye). Visual art aimed at a continuity between sensuous apprehension of surface and reference to a sensuous world. Its bodiliness, its immanence, its spatial presence, attracted Stevens as a cure for rhetoric. Of course no work of visual art achieves what it projects as its essence. The pure condition Stevens invokes belongs to the idea of painting rather than to its technique. What drew him to the theory of painting most of all, however, was its struggle to define the essence of its medium and its special relation to reality. The habit of broadly applying categories like "Cubism" or "Impressionism" (as Benamou does) proves particularly faulty with respect to Stevens' poetry. My argument falls between those who use the references to painting as an invitation to apply painterly categories to the poems, and those who read the references to painting as transparent metaphors for art, especially poetic art. They *are* metaphors, but as such they cannot be taken for granted.

Each reference to painting may have a local expedience. The "album of Corot" in "Like Decorations in a Nigger Cemetery," for instance, may suggest the special quality of nostalgia captured in Corot's "Souvenir de Montefontaine" or any other of his "souvenir" paintings. The reference to "the world seen through arches" in "Botanist on Alp (No. 1)" recalls the rock arches that appear repeatedly in Claude's paintings and suggests the entire concept of framed and idealized vision in Claude. But taken together, these allusions indicate a significant impulse in Stevens to associate his art with that of painting, and often suggest an ideal of realization appropriate to the sister art. Although Stevens' poems abound in references to particular artists and their works, it is finally the idea or ideal of painting, its struggle to define an imaginative space with a presence to rival natural experience, that attracts him; and in the transfer to his own verbal medium, the idea of painting becomes a poetic one, "not to be realized" but always imagined.

Fred Miller Robinson's essay, "Poems that Took the Place of Mountains: Realization in Stevens and Cézanne," is particularly helpful in understanding the distinction between an artist's ideals and his methods.[6] The struggle for realization that motivated Cézanne was by definition never satisfied, just as Stevens' "supreme fiction" remains an imaginative goal. But more than a parallel is involved here. Stevens often thought of the struggle for realization in terms of the enterprise of painting, even though he never attempted to imitate the methods of painting.

Stevens' essay, "The Relations between Poetry and Painting," provides little help on this subject; any art could fit the loose terms of his comparison. Stevens identifies no techniques of painting that poets might employ, no influence of one artist on another. The essay moves toward erasing difference by invoking the larger category "art," which he renames "poetry." But this renaming does matter, for it preserves the sense of difference that he cannot erase. The essay, written from the point of view of poetry, defines a certain attitude toward the visual arts. Indeed, he nearly sidesteps painting as such by claiming that poets find the "sayings" about painting useful. The essay at first might seem better named "The Relations between Poetry and Art Theory," or as Stevens says,

"the relations between poetry in paint and poetry in words." Criticism
and theory are inherently closer to poetry than to painting, since in the
first case the medium of language is shared. Indeed, the very analogy
between the arts is, in a sense, a literary trope. But Stevens cannot assimilate painting into poetry. Its point of view lingers to change the atmosphere of the poetic by associating it with "composition," as opposed to
"sensibility." Even the sayings of painters do not escape the conditions
from which they arise, but bring them along when they are associated
with poetry. This contagion – the contagion of analogy, not of imitation
– is my subject.

A better preface to this subject than Stevens' own is Walter Pater's
"The School of Giorgione," which Stevens probably read.[7] Pater begins
with a primary differentiation among the arts in terms of media: "That
the sensuous material of each art brings with it a special phase or quality
of beauty, untranslatable into the forms of any other, an order of impressions distinct in kind – is the beginning of all aesthetic criticism." (R 102)
The goal of each art is to purify itself in order to achieve this "special
phase or quality of beauty." Painting, for instance, should rid itself of
literature, which for Pater means discursiveness and rhetoricity, and aim
at pictoriality. Yet, paradoxically, "in its special mode of handling its
given material, each art may be observed to pass into the condition of
some other art" (R 106). Pater maintains a distinction between the medium
and the condition of each art, a distinction Stevens adapts. By "medium"
Pater means, for example, the material of paint and the techniques developed for handling that material. By "condition" he means each art's special mode of reaching the imagination, its representational structure and
its "special mode or quality of beauty." These are inseparable but not
identical for Pater, as for Stevens; but that does not prevent a given art
from invoking the condition of another through its own particular
medium. The Paterian crossing of the arts involves a "partial alienation
[of an art] from its own limitations, through which the arts are able, not
indeed to supply the place of each other but reciprocally to lend each
other new forces" (R 105). In this view the purity of the arts and the
exchange between the arts are not at odds. Indeed, in praising Giorgione's school for realizing its goals within pictorial form, Pater calls
their work "pictorial poetry." "They belong to a sort of poetry which
tells itself without an articulated story." (R 117) It is in this spirit, perhaps, that Stevens speaks of the poetry of impressionism.

And it is in this spirit that Stevens speaks, conversely, in "Effects of
Analogy," of pictorialization as the essential aim of poetry.[8] Although
describing a distinctly rhetorical device – analogy – he expresses his frus-
tration with the limitations of language, which he, following Pater, iden-

tifies with discursiveness and rhetoricity. Allegory, in particular, is the enemy. True analogy promises a "consummation" (NA 114) of terms – not the pictorialization of descriptions or emblemata, but an objectification of imagination. Stevens writes, "The effect of analogy is the effect of the degree of appositeness . . . the imaginative projection, the imaginative deviation, raises the question of rightness, as if in the vast association of ideas there existed for every object its appointed objectification. In such a case, the object and its image become inseparable." (NA 114) At the end of the essay Stevens explicitly calls the structure of analogy itself a "pictorialization" – though he means the word figuratively, as restatement or illustration. It is clear nonetheless that the visual remains the touchstone of figuration for him. In this way the analogy between poetry and painting becomes for Stevens a meta-analogy. In seeking for the essence of poetry Stevens distances himself from its limitations, and by invoking painting in various ways he borrows new forces. The limitations inherent in literature – its inescapable discursiveness and rhetoricity, what Paul de Man would call its inescapably allegorical nature – make a place in Stevens' imagination for painting. Stevens identifies analogy as emotional in origin: "The nature of the image is analogous with the emotion from which it springs." (NA 111) If we take painting itself (as opposed to this painting or that) as a major analogy, we may identify it with an emotion everywhere in Stevens – a yearning for the conditions of immanence, unity, presentness, and the incarnation of imagination in materiality.

Anterior to the metaphor of painting in Stevens is the very privileged metaphor of the eye, which is more than a substitute term for consciousness of reality. Stevens' development reflects his ambivalence about the eye's domination of consciousness, but it remains a determinant and touchstone. The figure – the agent of the eye – haunts all conceptualization. He tells us in "Crude Foyer" that "the eye is the mind," and in "Fishscale Sunrise" that "the mind is smaller than the eye."[9] And yet the imagination must experience some freedom from the eye to validate itself. In addressing this central problem, painting offered a direction – a liberation from visual reality that nevertheless made a truce with the eye. Stevens' attraction to painting is based, in part, on his alienation from the very rhetoricity and discursiveness so dominant in his own poetry. The visual thinking of painters suggested direct access to a space in which the world might find its imaginative apposite. The language of poetry, at least as Stevens employed it, might gesture toward that space, but could not create it. On the other hand, Stevens saw the figurative as the root of all thought, and embodiment as its irreducible condition. The reimagined first idea, then, must be a figure, not its dependent theory or thought. Painting not only suggested a path to immanence not available in poetry (at least in the highly discursive and rhetorical poetry of Wallace Stevens), it also seemed truer as an imitation of thought.

In arguing that Stevens' poetry expresses a yearning for the condition of the visual arts I must acknowledge that he occasionally links painting and poetry as two different forms of rhetoric, opposing them to nature. But the distinction between reality and its representations in Stevens is far less significant than the distinction between what he calls "evading metaphor" and "figure," the latter somehow achieving immanence where the former only removes the beholder from the presence of nature. In "Add This to Rhetoric" Stevens begins by distinguishing between being in nature – simple growth – and the arrangement of being through language. He treats painting and speech together here as forms of rhetoric, using painting as an analogy for the "posed" and "framed" aspect of speech:

> The buildings pose in the sky
> and, as you paint, the clouds,
> Grisaille, impearled, profound,
> Pfft. . . . In the way you speak
> You arrange, the thing is posed,
> What in nature merely grows.

Here Stevens suggests that the intervention of "rhetoric" determines the structure of perception itself, so that the "thing" in its natural state of growth remains elusive. Even "stones pose in the falling night." As he so often does, Stevens divides the worlds of imagination and reality, of rhetoric and nature, into moonlight and sunlight. As the sun comes up in the second stanza, a new authenticity of being promises to rise with it:

> To-morrow when the sun,
> For all your images,
> Comes up as the sun, bull fire,
> Your images will have left
> No shadow of themselves.
> The poses of speech, of paint,
> Of music – Her body lies
> Worn out, her arm falls down,
> Her fingers touch the ground.
> Above her, to the left,
> A brush of white, the obscure,
> The moon without a shape,
> A fringed eye in a crypt.

The sense creates the pose.
In this it moves and speaks.
This is the figure and not
An evading metaphor.

Add this. It is to add.

The second stanza seems to contrast with the first by suggesting a refreshed vision of reality against the decay of old images. But the image that lies suspended in the poem no longer contrasts nature and its poses. The distinction is now rather between figure and evading metaphor. Stevens does not spell out the difference between these terms, but together they suggest his desire to reserve a region of immanence within representation. The "figure" is clearly a visual concept, for the corresponding image is a tableau ("Above her, to the left,"). Within that tableau, however, we see the erasure of the figure – the "fringed eye in a crypt" and "the moon without a shape." Stevens here approaches the nexus between sense and transcendence within a visual vocabulary.

Stevens' poems constantly search for a reimagining, a representation that will be free of the touch of rhetoric or will achieve "the pure rhetoric of a language without words." Metaphor, as a substitute, removes the imaginer from the immediate experience. The figure promises something less shadowy, more substantial, and thus more immediate. Thus to add the figure to rhetoric would be to make rhetoric more real. But the final line of the poem reinstates Stevens' ambivalence about all representation. "It is to add" might as easily be taken as an expression of disappointment, for an addition is not a transformation. Stevens remains insecure in his belief in the power of the figure, his "supreme fiction." But the poem indicates at least his need to define the space of authenticity not outside or beyond but within representation. Stevens' allusions to painting helped him develop this special place for the figure in opposition to evading metaphor – helped him sustain, that is, an idealized project for art.

In *Harmonium,* as many have noted, Stevens expresses his visual intensity through images. Michel Benamou has suggested that "Sunday Morning" evokes Matisse; Helen Vendler finds a source in Manet's "Woman with a Parrot," acquired by the Metropolitan Museum of Art in New York in 1866 (Figure 1). In "Sunday Morning" we enter an interior life through a contrast of surface intensity and blur, just as in Manet areas of detail work against rough, impressionistic ones. Poem and painting share the woman in peignoir, the orange, and the overall suggestion of sensuous pleasure recently enjoyed against a somber, meditative background. If the painting is a source of the poem, the parrot has

Figure 1. Eduard Manet, "Woman with a Parrot." Metropolitan Museum of Art, New York. Gift of Erwin Davis, 1889.

been transplanted to the rug and given the more poetic name "cockatoo," as if to create a verbal equivalent to Manet's visual exoticism. But "Sunday Morning" does not dwell on this initial image or on any other; it veers off into interior dialogue, into areas to which poetry has privileged access. We are quickly thwarted if we try to match Stevens' poems to particular visual sources. While "Sea Surface Full of Clouds" is also strikingly imagistic, its transformations, suggesting one of Monet's series, are driven as much by linguistic as by visual elements. The poem never truly depicts anything. Stevens seemed to discover in this early book that poetry could never aim at the quality of painting through pictoriality, and the image recedes in later volumes. Yet the metaphors of painting (of which there are few in *Harmonium*) increase dramatically in *Parts of a World*.

In "Poem Written at Morning" (CP 219), for instance, Stevens insistently identifies the enterprises of poetry and painting:

> A sunny day's complete Poussiniana
> Divide it from itself. It is this or that
> And it is not.
>   By metaphor you paint
> A thing.

But as the poem goes on, a certain differentiation emerges between the terms metaphor and paint, and with that difference a sense of lack in each, a vacillating preference. The identification raises problems in the later repetition of "The senses paint by metaphor." This phrasing still sets painting as the end or desired condition, metaphor as the means, making the poem tautological. Painting is never aimed at metaphor. We do not, that is, have a corollary concept by which transcendence is achieved through a visual immediacy. Yet to paint, in this poem, means not only to render visible but to give the world a certain aspect, a certain emotional cast or conceptual character. Paint, then, becomes an end rather than a means, while metaphor remains a means. The poem begins with a condition of painting and divides it from itself in metaphor, in order to return to a condition of painting ("by metaphor you paint a thing"). One would expect this poem to begin with the "thing" itself, but the thing is already represented in the first line, so that the accomplishment of painting is given originating power. "A sunny day's complete Poussiniana" describes less the rhetoricity of a day which is completely Poussin-like than the completeness of effect, the immanence and autonomy achieved by Poussin, so that nature and Poussin are the same, as nature and Homer were to Pope.

But perhaps uncomfortable with the priority of painting, the poem moves away from its initial subject to analyze a thing, a pineapple. As the poem continues, that full presence earlier described as "a sunny day's complete Poussiniana" gives way to something more elusive:

> Thus, the pineapple was a leather fruit,
> A fruit for pewter, thorned and palmed and blue,
> To be served by men of ice.
> > The senses paint
> By metaphor. The juice was fragranter
> Than wettest cinnamon.

The metaphors are not pictorial, but engage all the senses toward a conceptualization of the object. Poetry, it seems to suggest, is not bound to one sensuous aspect and is thus "truer" because it can conceptualize by a chorus of all:

> The truth must be
> That you do not see, you experience, you feel,
> That the buxom eye brings merely its element
> To the total thing.

Yet the "total thing" is lost, indeed chased away by metaphor, to become "a shapeless giant forced upward." We no longer have the timeless or at least tenseless (the first line having no temporal designation) completeness of the sunny day's Poussiniana, but a mere epitaph: The poem ends, "Green were the curls upon that head." It is hard to find the balance in adding the debits and credits of each art.

If we take the poem's argument as a narrative, the introduction of metaphor into the poem is connected with the advent of time and loss. Painting, then, is identified with a tenseless spatiality; but this is a poem, marked in its title as temporally burdened. The end of the poem denies the privilege of the eye as access to completeness. But painting of course involves more than the eye, is itself metaphoric, just as metaphor is figurative. The final effect is both a merging and an ambivalence. Perhaps Stevens is deconstructing Poussin's illusion of completeness. Or perhaps he is trying to have it both ways by his surface identification. But internally the poem expresses nostalgia for the figurative power of painting even while it deconstructs that power.

Of course in reading the poem in this way I place extra weight on the word "paint" and on the fact of Poussin's medium. One could try to ignore these details and read the poem as a contrast between classical illusionism and modern conceptualization, between Poussin and Juan Gris, or equivalently between Racine and Stevens. The pineapple was a favorite Cubist motif, and the attempt of some Cubists was to liberate painting from the tyranny of the eye. Stevens quotes Juan Gris in "The Relations between Poetry and Painting" as giving the imagination priority over the visual, and quotes Braque's aphorism, "The senses deform, the

Figure 2. Nicholas Poussin, "Spring." The Louvre, Paris. Print from Musées Nationaux.

mind forms" (NA 161). Conversely, in the same essay, he identifies Poussin with Racine. But "a sunny day's complete Raciniana" or even "Virgiliana" would have a very different effect in the poem. It is the pictoriality of Poussin that matters here, a condition for which literature has no substitute, but from which it is always borrowing.

The poem's structure, from completeness to division, from painting to metaphor, from presence to absence, suggests a concept of the Fall for which the poem may have an iconographic source. The iconographic reading of the poem, that is, reinforces its aesthetic argument. Stevens may have been thinking of Poussin's "Spring," which depicts Eden's completeness of ripe fruit before its harvest (Figure 2). Iconography provides the most literal kind of association with literature, but in its sensuous immediacy and incarnation of meaning maintains a difference from language that might have appealed to Stevens. Iconography helps define the difference between figure and evading metaphor. Like Keats, his major precursor, Stevens recognizes the special power of the visual arts to preserve ephemeral subjects. The sunny day is complete in Poussin even if in nature or narration it must decline.

"The Common Life" (CP 221) offers another example of how poetry borrows rather than copies the pictoriality of the visual arts. The poem seems to be describing something visual (perhaps a work by Klee, who often plays with verbal and visual signs on a single surface), but no distinct pictorial image emerges:

> That's the down-town frieze,
> Principally the church steeple,
> A black line beside a white line;
> And the stack of the electric plant,
> A black line drawn on flat air.

Instead of organizing one visual focus, the image, as we shall see, undergoes a metamorphosis, from landscape to geometric drawing to text. The subject holding these images together is "the common life": the dreariness of the common, but perhaps also the abstractness of the common. (In that second sense the term "common" is no longer pejorative.) On a primary level all the images serve to reinforce this subject, suggesting absence of color, third dimension, movement, particularity, vitality. But the two metaphors also modify each other so that the qualities of drawing (spatiality, line, background) combine with qualities of textuality (print, page, volume). Toward the end of the poem we begin to imagine the graphic aspects of a book through a subtle punning on the words "volume" and "outline" that conflates visual and textual categories:

> The paper is whiter
> For these black lines.
> It glares beneath the webs
> Of wire, the designs of ink,
> The planes that ought to have genius,
> The volumes like marble ruins
> Outlined and having alphabetical
> Notations and footnotes.

Textual abstraction takes on a kind of materiality by its identification with visual abstraction. And the discursive and rhetorical aspect of the poem yields to the immediacy of the figure. By the end of the poem the referential subject has disappeared almost completely, supplanted by the figure of the text.

I have been discussing examples that invoke the visual arts for their privileged *figurative* power. The poems do not attempt to simulate the graphic presence of visual art, but import it into the poem by association. This loyalty to literary method is most apparent in the many poems which tell the story of a beholder. The reader does not share in the act of beholding, but rather in its interpretation, in the story of the beholder's consciousness. Stevens thus utilizes poetry's privileged *interpretive* power, its temporal dimension and its special access to mental conditions. But the terms of the interpretation often suggest the motivations and feelings appropriate to the enterprise of painting. (Only in this sense does the Picasso connection in "The Man with the Blue Guitar" make sense.)[10] That is, an objectification (as opposed to interpretation) of such experience would be visual rather than verbal.

This highly speculative claim is supported by the titles of these poems about beholders, which often imitate the titles of paintings: "Landscape with Boat," "Botanist on Alp (No. 1)," "Botanist on Alp (No. 2)," "Woman Looking at a Vase of Flowers," "Bouquet of Roses in Sunlight." While titles are the most literary component of painting, these in particular suggest distinctly painterly subjects and approaches. Since they have little narrative or conceptual implication – as opposed to, say, "Anecdote of the Jar" or "The Idea of Order at Key West" – they put the poems in a painter's space. Such titles provide visual foci to counterbalance the interiority of the subsequent discourse. But they are not iconographic, as are such titles as "Angel Surrounded by Paysans" (based on a painting Stevens owned) or "The Virgin Carrying a Lantern," which invite narrative and interpretation. Landscape and still life are the genres of those who place visual *above* literary values. Williams, again wishing to identify the effects of painting and poetry, argued in "Still Life" that the poised object bears within it a Homeric narrative.[11] But we do not "read" landscape or still life in any usual narrative sense. They declare a primary visual experience to which the poem will address itself. Stevens in this sense plants the enterprise of painting in the reader's mind when he describes the predicaments, successes, and failures of his beholders. The condition these poems either gesture toward or yearn for is the condition of visual epiphany, a wordless condition defined in opposition to discursiveness and rhetoricity. Their titles ask us to think of these poems in terms of design rather than statement, as ways of seeing rather than of saying. Such titles help to loose poetry from its dependence on statement. And yet that freedom remains, in Stevens, largely *hypothetical*. Discursiveness remains a dominant element in his compositions, an ordering principle.

"Botanist on Alp (No. 1)" (CP 134–35) clearly asks us to consider the place of painting in culture, indeed measures other ways of ordering (the botanists' taxonomic realism, Marxist historicism and materialism) against the achievement of painting. Of course it is not painting in general, but Claude's painting, especially his integrations of nature and architectural ruin, that offered an ideal. Still, Claude's precedent and the title together suggest that Modernism might seek its appropriate order in this medium.

Against the incursions of materialism and historicism any art promises a sustaining, timeless, and elevating vision, but perhaps visual art best of all because it combines materiality and imagination. The "poem" in "Botanist on Alp (No. 2)" (CP 135–36) does not offer an order but a compensatory or consolatory accompaniment to the vision of the "crosses glittering." This is a search for sustaining vision, not sustaining utterance. Virgil could not easily substitute for Claude in "Botanist on Alp (No. 1)."

> But in Claude how near one was
> (In a world that was resting on pillars,
> That was seen through arches)
> To the central composition,
> The essential theme.

But the painting prescribed by the title is, of course, an impossible one, or at least a ridiculous one. The botanist is incapable of the sublime, incapable of composition: "Corridors of cloudy thoughts, / Seem pretty much one: / I don't know what." Still, the modern problem as it is posed here seems more than metaphorically a problem of seeing, which suggests that solutions might be sought on a visual plane.

"Landscape with Boat" (CP 241–43) similarly uses a title to mark the absence of a successful act of beholding. Stevens' negations are the negations of painting.[12] In place of the old master is the antimaster (as Marx replaced Claude), who refuses "any turquoise tint or phase, / Any azure under-side or after-color." Instead of brushing on, he brushes away the thunder, undoing illusion. We have only the hint of an image at the end, as the northern abstractive mentality yields to the Mediterranean sensory allure. Of course painting is a metaphor here; but it is precisely my point that metaphors cannot be taken for granted, that they change our attitude toward a subject. The failure of the ascetic's vision is a failure of the eye.

The problem of Modernism's negations (especially Cubist negations) is again the subject of "Study of Two Pears," whose title clearly invokes visual art. The concerns of the body of the poem – shape, color, outline, resemblance – also derive from painting. As does Cubist painting, the poem suggests both a struggle to see reality as it is and to create an imaginative reality. The poem ends ironically, for while the pears are not seen as the observer wills (not as viols, nudes, or bottles), it is only these willed images that *are* seen. The poem seems to move in this direction toward the last two stanzas where the reality of the pears is entirely elusive – a glistening at best. Even their shadows are only defined as "blobs on the green cloth." The dull, flat language of "Study of Two Pears" may reflect the dullness of bondage to visual fact. Such objectivism is only an "opusculum paedagogum." But the poem also perhaps testifies to the failure of language to represent adequately the allure of visual fact (it "glistens"). Without metaphor (without viols, nudes, or bottles) language is nothing, and yet metaphor implies an evasion, a removal from positive direct experience. Stevens' ambivalence about the eye centers, then, on his allusions to painting. Here his own stance as observer/describer seems inadequate to capture observation. The poem does not offer an equivalence in language to Cubist concerns and techniques, but rather a description of those concerns and techniques, a substitution rather than an apposition.

In bringing together poetry and painting as he does, Stevens attempts to fuse the visible and the invisible in a most uncompromising fashion. His name for that fusion is the figure. "Woman Looking at a Vase of Flowers" (CP 246–47) and "Bouquet of Roses in Sunlight" (CP 430–31) tell the story of successful vision, in which the senses take their place in cooperation with imagination, figuration is achieved, and rhetoricity is escaped without cost to subjectivity. In both these poems Stevens associates the focal moment of beholding with painting; but he uses the body of each poem to narrate and interpret rather than to duplicate this moment.

"Woman Looking at a Vase of Flowers" is a lyric accompaniment to a visual event. The poet narrates the interior space of the beholder, a space taken up with the act of seeing. The little owl within her may hoot, but she herself is silent. The title directs our attention to the mute picture, but the devices of the poem are conspicuously literary. "It was as if" generates the poem. The terms of comparison are entirely relational rather than substantive, so they can shift position in the rhetorical structure of analogy: "The wind dissolving into birds . . . / . . . the sea poured out again/ In east wind beating the shutters at night." The duality of approach, the combinatory nature of analogy, is emphasized repeatedly against the *unity* of the act of looking. And the narrative tells of something in the past, an event that once occurred – "it *was*," as against the continuous present of the "woman looking." While the narrative is anticipatory and recollective, the woman's experience fills the moment. Without consciousness of time, "without clairvoyance," she is caught up in the gaze. The metaphors introduce an analogy with painting, with the movement from palette to canvas to illusion:

> High blue became particular
> In leaf and bud and how the red,
> Flicked into pieces, points of air,
> Became – how the central, essential red
> Escaped its large abstraction

Even without a concept of the divine, the concept of sensous reality remains intentional, the incarnation of idea into visual medium:

> the inhuman colors fell
> Into place beside her, where she was,
> Like human conciliations, more like
> A profounder reconciling, an act,
> An affirmation free from doubt.

The artist is not present here, but in a sense the beholder embodies the artist while she distances the act of creation. One almost feels that in conceiving this poem Stevens circled back into a pictorial process, inferring from an image an original formless condition of color-idea from which the image was generated or "flicked" like a brush. The argument by design without a concept of God invites the idea of the beholder as painter. While the "vase of flowers" is the object beheld, it is also, perhaps, the counterpart of the woman's imagination, which gathers and arranges the scattered particulars of nature into a visual order.

"Bouquet of Roses in Sunlight" again uses literary means to express a condition of beholding that only painting can approach. Again there is little here that can be called pictorial – the discursiveness of the poem advertises itself in syllogistic rhetoric ("say that," "and yet," "so"), presenting and redefining oppositions. Yet the condition it describes is one of apparent freedom from rhetoricity. The very directive voice of the poem stands in opposition to the condition of freedom it dictates. That is, while the poem's method of understanding is literary, the mode of understanding it wishes us to conceive is more atuned to the visual arts – color as feeling; presymbolic sensation rooted in unconscious emotion; direct unity of sensation and imagination. Stevens emphasizes that this experience is still a reimagining – a seeming, not an objectification – but it has a quality of immanence, of meaning inherent in an act of looking. The suggestion of painting begins at the outset, not only with the title, but with the notion of visual "effect" – black reds, pink yellows, orange whites, and so forth: a reality of color. Further, the experience here is of "meaning with no speech," transformation through sense and not through metaphor that seems "beyond the rhetorician's touch." The objectification of a reimagining without the evasions of metaphor, without rhetoric, is *the figure,* the primary condition of painting.

The seeing of reality as artistic creation is one subject of "Holiday in Reality" (CP 312–13), in which Stevens begins as a beholder in a gallery, finds it stifling, and then enters an imagined garden, a "green world." In the gallery Stevens meditates on the work of a northern consciousness, on paintings such as the snowman, not Cézanne, might likely produce:

It was something to see that their white was different
Sharp as white paint in the January sun;

Something to feel that they needed another yellow,
Less Aix than Stockholm, hardly a yellow at all,

A vibrancy not to be taken for granted, from
A sun in an almost colorless, cold heaven.

Stevens pretends at first to reserve judgment on these artists ("It was
something to see"), but then goes on to identify their conceptual failings:

Why should they not know they had everything of their own
As each had a particular woman and her touch?

Their desire to depersonalize vision is, for Stevens, at odds with the drama
of beholding. Although attracted to the ambition of this art, he finds its
results stifling: "It is impossible to breathe at Durand-Ruel's." Like the
gloriously subjective figure in "Tea at the Palaz of Hoon," Stevens declares
in the second half of the poem that the objects of nature "are real only if
I make them so"; yet as the imagination dictates reality, the objects it
creates take on the quality of otherness and unreality and are seen "more
truly and more strange":

Whistle
For me, grow green for me and, as you whistle and grow
    green,

Intangible arrows quiver and stick in the skin
And I taste at the root of the tongue the unreal of what is real.

It should be observed that this taste of reality is not entirely pleasant
("Intangible arrows quiver and stick in the skin"). The garden is clearly
an Eden that can fall, not an immortal world of white paint. The structure of the poem superficially suggests a division between art and reality,
but the sense of reality itself emerges as the moment of strangeness in the
imagination's conjuring (like Marianne Moore's real toad in the imaginary garden). Reality is, in a sense, a product of creative imagination.
Thus it is a "holiday" rather than a norm. The division is rather between
two types of art – the snowman's art of pristine, ascetic vision and the
southerly art (of Cézanne?) that welcomes the spirit's participation in
perception.

The poems I have been discussing all demonstrate the Paterian condition of alienation from the limitations of one's art form. Like Pater, Stevens invokes the sister art in such a way as to maintain the integrity of

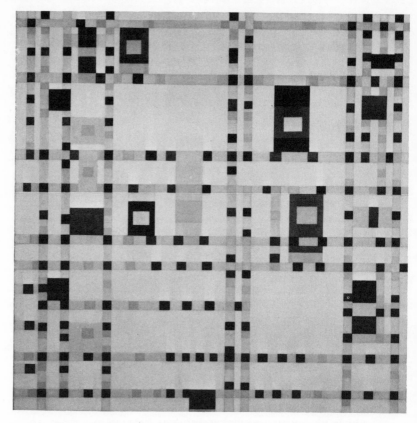

Figure 3. Piet Mondrian, "Broadway Boogie Woogie," 1942–43, oil on canvas, 50 by 50 in. Collection, The Museum of Modern Art, New York.

his fostering art. The moments of visual epiphany indeed seem to pass into the condition of painting: exceeding verbality, filled with colors and shapes not reducible to symbolic counterwords. It is not surprising that when the hero of "The Latest Freed Man" (CP 204–205) escapes "doctrine" or feels that he has, he approaches visual epiphany; his eye lights on objects with little narrative or interpretive potential – a rug, a chair, a picture. Indeed, he sees a "portrait of Vidal"; the *art* dealer, Vidal, "qui fait fi des jolliesses banales," who said "fi" to pretty banalities, becomes for a moment the figure of major man.

Thus far the conditions of painting that I have mentioned are located in illusionistic representation; but Stevens also greatly admired the achievements of several abstract artists, particularly Klee, Mondrian, and Brancusi. These artists escaped derivativeness and displayed an ideal

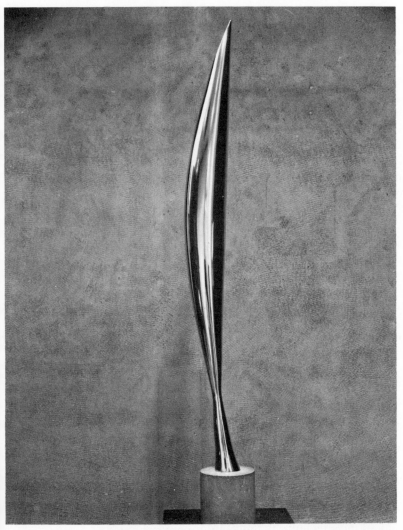

Figure 4. Constantin Brancusi, "Bird in Space," 1928(?), bronze (unique cast), 54 in. high. Collection, The Museum of Modern Art, New York.

commitment to abstraction. To Barbara Church, Stevens wrote that Arp lacks "integrity as an abstractionist" but that "for Mondrian the abstract was the abstract" (CL 628). (See Figure 3.) And two days later, to Thomas McGreevy: "Arp is fastidious not forceful. His forms will never consti- tute a 'visionary language.' Unlike Brancusi they never intimidate one with their possibilities." (CL 629). (See Figure 4.) Intimidation before the possibilities of a "visionary language" suggested in certain works of art is exactly the theme of "Notes toward a Supreme Fiction" with its challenging dictum, "It must be abstract." In rejecting naïve anthropomorphic and organic values (such as he finds in Arp and complains about in "Notes") Stevens evokes painting once again: "The air is not a mirror but bare board, / Coulisse bright-dark, tragic chiaroscuro." (CP 384) Since the world is not a reflection of ourselves, since we "live in a world that is not our own," we must invent one, the poem insists. That "invented world" is nonobjective, but still, in a sense, visually representable. Although he declares it is "Not to be realized because not to / Be seen," it is nevertheless through a visual artist that Stevens gains access to his subject. "Weather by Franz Hals" is, for Stevens, abstract, "brushed up by brushy winds in brushy clouds, / Wetted by blue, colder for white." The supreme fiction

> must be visible or invisible,
> Invisible or visible or both:
> A seeing and unseeing in the eye.

Hals represents clouds that "preceded us." (They stand in the background of his portraits, and Stevens seems to read them as a kind of first condition out of which human identity, the being of the portrait, emerges.) But this "weather," this "mere air" is "an abstraction blooded, as a man by thought." Abstraction remains "in the eye" even if invisible, an ideal of embodiment without loss of sublimity. Abstraction is not itself a "thought" separable from image. One would expect thought to be aligned with abstraction, but Stevens' syntax identifies thought with blood, with something embodied and concrete. If thought is blood, if the first idea is not a mere abstraction, then perhaps the hermit in the poet's metaphors, the first idea or first condition of things, is, after all, the irreducible figurative aspect of thought, which painting, especially abstract painting, addresses. The figuration of abstract painting seems to do without the "as if," without the structure of substitution on which rhetoric relies. It brings the alien, abstract first idea, the condition of the clouds, into the realm of the intelligible without anthropomorphism.

Stevens everywhere explores the idea that the sister arts are pulled together by the ambitions and latent tendencies of each. Just as a latent textuality haunts all visual images, so a latent figurativeness haunts all discourse. Stevens inherited from Pater (and later from Valéry) a desire for purity in the arts, but also a sense of their deep reciprocity. We have been exploring the associations of painting imported into Stevens' poetry by literary means. His writing on art completes this reciprocity. Just as Pater wrote of the "poetry" of the School of Giorgione, so Stevens writes of a work by Raoul Dufy that "it is an exploitation of fact by a man of elevation. It is a surface of prose changeable with the luster of poetry and thought."[13] Yet these are artists who, for Stevens, achieve their "poetic" quality in pursuit of, not in betrayal of, the essence of their medium, recalling the Paterian paradox. It is in pursuit of that essence that Stevens' poetry passes into the condition of the visual arts.

NOTES

1   *The Letters of Wallace Stevens,* ed. Holly Stevens (New York: Knopf, 1966), p. 671. Subsequent references in text, abbreviated *L.*

2   Michel Benamou, *Wallace Stevens and the Symbolist Imagination* (Princeton: Princeton University Press, 1972).

3   William Carlos Williams, "An Interview with William Carlos Williams," conducted by Walter Sutton, 1961, in *Interviews with William Carlos Williams,* ed. Linda Wagner (New York: New Directions, 1976), p. 53.

4   Bram Djikstra, *Hieroglyphics of a New Speech: Cubism, Stieglitz and the Early Poetry of William Carlos Williams* (Princeton: Princeton University Press, 1969); Henry Sayre, *The Visual Text of William Carlos Williams* (Champaign: University of Illinois Press, 1983). See also my own article, "William Carlos Williams in a World of Painters," *New Boston Review* (June/July 1979).

5   Quoted in Wallace Stevens, "The Relations between Poetry and Painting," in *The Necessary Angel: Essays on Reality and the Imagination* (New York: Random House, 1951), pp. 159–76.

6   Fred Miller Robinson, "Poems that Took the Place of Mountains: Realization in Stevens and Cézanne," *The Centennial Review* 22 (1978), 281–98.

7   Walter Pater, *The Renaissance: Studies in Art and Poetry* (Berkeley: University of California Press, 1980), pp. 102–22. Subsequent references will be made in text, abbreviated R.

8   Wallace Stevens, "Effects of an Analogy," in *The Necessary Angel,* p. 129. Subsequent references will be noted in text, abbreviated NA.

9   Wallace Stevens, *The Collected Poems of Wallace Stevens* (New York: Knopf, 1954): "Crude Foyer," p. 305; "Fish-scale Sunrise," p. 161. Subsequent references will be made in text, abbreviated CP.

10 For a full discussion of this connection see Judith Rinde Sheridan, "The Picasso Connection: Wallace Stevens' 'Man with the Blue Guitar'," *Arizona Quarterly* 35 (1979), 77–89.

11 For a discussion of Williams' "Still Life" see Costello, "William Carlos Williams in a World of Painters," p. 11.

12 For a discussion of negation in Modernist painting (especially in Marxist terms) see T. J. Clark, "Clement Greenberg's Theory of Art," *Critical Inquiry* 9 (1982), 134–56. Clark's argument bears an interesting resemblance to Stevens' in "Landscape with Boat."

13 Wallace Stevens, *Opus Posthumous: Poems, Plays, Prose,* ed. Samuel French Morse (New York: Knopf, 1957), p. 286.

5

Why Stevens Must Be Abstract, or What a Poet Can Learn from Painting

CHARLES ALTIERI

I

One need not be Harold Bloom to find something oddly proleptic in the way Wallace Stevens casts his imperative, "It must be abstract." For it is probably only under the dispensation of the suspicious impulse now dominating contemporary literary criticism that the force of Stevens' imaginings could become fully clear. This is not to say, of course, that the proponents of such criticism would find Stevens convincing. They would want to know what his imperatives conceal: How does abstraction allow him to escape or to perpetuate certain social conditions, to reinforce certain roles, or to evade problems threatening other interests? The most sensitive of the new historicists would also recognize their own suspicions as perhaps expressing a profound cultural shift which has made it difficult even to entertain seriously those questions Stevens inherited from Romanticism. Yet too programmatic and generalized a commitment to these demystifying inquiries renders the critics more suspect than Stevens himself. What do they expect of poets, and why do they so rely on political critiques without confronting Stevens' deliberate rejection of the political order? Do they perhaps suppress out of embarrassment any need to take responsibility for their own idealizations? And might the commitment to suspicion derive in large part from their method having no language by which to take seriously what writers think they have to offer? What else can result when critics find it essential to close-read for how a poet evades reality, yet insist that it is nostalgic to close-read as a way of seeing just what claims on the real a poet's conscious manipulation of language can project?[1]

I do not raise these issues to escalate a war among competing pieties. Rather my primary (conscious) interest is to set as a context for Stevens our own involvement in the feelings and questions he saw as exemplars of "the pressure of reality" on modern life. When we see our "devotions" as defined by that critical spirit, we may be more willing to listen to Stevens before we allow ourselves the pleasures of trying to be superior to him. This critical spirit, however powerful, exacts a substantial cost that we can perhaps avoid if we develop a significant counterpressure showing the value of poets who imagine their function as becoming "the light in the minds of others . . . to help people live their lives."[2] For that case I want to concentrate on what Stevens makes of the imperative to abstraction because his work in this vein adapts to its purposes the fundamental principles of the Modernist revolution established by the visual arts, thereby also establishing significant parallels to the philosophical enterprise of minimalist assertion typified by Wittgenstein.

II

It is no accident that Stevens' clearest definition of abstraction follows directly upon his clearest definition of the pressure of reality. Modernist abstraction provides a model of human agency whose force depends in large part on its capacity to resist the model causing that pressure. Stevens' antagonist is the ideal of demystification produced by the Enlightenment dream which locates nobility in a lucid spirit capable of judging even itself in unsentimental third-person terms.[3] To count as knowledge, statements must refer to demonstrable phenomena and codify them under generalizations that subordinate subjective intentions to determinate processes. Such lucidity dreams of expunging everything that claims mystery or "edification" for itself on the basis of privileged first-person testimony. Eventually this lucidity would turn its lens on itself, showing that its own ideal must itself be understood as caused and hence as not continuous with any straightforward principle allowing us somehow to choose an identity. We arrive by default at an infinite suspicion, perennially uneasy about the very imperatives that justify it. The only psychology our theories can trust (as opposed, I think, to what our practices in fact rely on) is one founded on distrust. Seen from a third-person perspective, our actions only make sense as the pursuit of concealed interests and chances to dominate. And our theories of meaning must reflect positivist dichotomies between demonstrable certainties and endless slippage caught up in the deferring play of desire. For Stevens, then, the pressure of reality leaves the imagination "always at the end of an era" (NA 22). The imagination's desires to use first-person experience as a test for its idealizations keep it continuously vulnerable to demystification, a victim of the very needs it tries to assuage. So long as we try to believe in its products, we find ourselves generating fictions ultimately doomed to become the dead metaphors cluttering history's junk heap. Eventually we contaminate any sense of our own power to do other than become perpetual ironists.

This sense of the demands on modernity is common to all the heirs of Hegel – from William James, to Adorno, to Derrida. Stevens is distinctive, though, in the specific strategies by which he hopes to exert counterpressure. He turns to the constructive powers of the mind, hoping to be abstract enough to separate powers in which one can believe from the specific contents that history undoes. The first gesture that "The Noble Rider and the Sound of Words" proposes against its account of the pressure of reality is a self-conscious act of the imagination turning to its own idealizing capacities: "Suppose we try, now to construct the figure of a poet, or possible poet" (NA 23). In the poet's construction of his own functions you will know him and begin to see how such abstractions can reach levels not subsumable under specific historical postivities. Stevens' subsequent argument can be reconstructed from the following composite of quotations:

> He will wonder at those huge imaginations, in which what is remote becomes near, and what is dead lives with an intensity beyond any experience of life. He will consider that although he has himself witnessed, during the long period of his life, a general transition to reality, his own measure as a poet, in spite of all the passions of all the lovers of truth, is the measure of his power to abstract himself, and to withdraw with him into his abstraction the reality on which the lovers of truth insist. He must be able to abstract himself and also to abstract reality, which he does by placing it in his imagination. . . . [By this process we come to see] the imagination and reality equal and inseparable. (NA 22–23) The subject matter of poetry is not that "collection of solid static objects extended in space" but the life that is lived in the scene that it composes; and so reality is not that external scene but the life that is lived in it. Reality is things as they are. (NA 25) The imagination gives to everything that it touches a peculiarity, and it seems to me that the peculiarity of the imagination is nobility, of which there are many degrees. . . . I mean that nobility which is our spiritual height and depth. (NA 33) There is no element more conspicuously absent from contemporary poetry than nobility. . . . The nobility of rhetoric is of course, a lifeless nobility. Pareto's epigram that history is a cemetery of aristocracies easily becomes another: that poetry is a

cemetery of nobilities. For the sensitive poet, conscious of negations, nothing is more difficult than the affirmations of nobility
and yet there is nothing that he requires of himself more persistently. (NA 35) As a wave is a force and not the water of which
it is composed, which is never the same, so nobility is a force
and not the manifestation of which it is composed . . . It is not
artifice that the mind has added to human nature . . . It is the
imagination pressing back against the pressure of reality. (NA
37)

Four principles are critical here for defining the powers and scope of
abstraction in poetry. First, abstraction is a means for poetry to make
disclosures about the world while setting itself against the pursuit of
propositions that can be judged for their truth as descriptions. Second,
abstraction is a contrary of "truth" because it has force as a process rather
than as a statement. Indeed, it can resist the pressure of reality precisely
because it can be opposed to all reification. Third, this process has claims
to be, or to account for reality, because the process per se can be seen as
occupying a particular site, that of the poem, where we in effect are
confronted with a display of our own powers. This site allows a way of
understanding processes which puts before us a sense of the self become
impersonal or transpersonal and rendered on a level where reification and
its resulting ideological forms can be evaded. The basic means for such
evasion is the fact that the life lived in the scene is one in which any
attentive reader can participate. Finally, these exercises in abstraction have
the important consequence of enabling us to display to ourselves human
powers and human relations to an environment with an intensity that
warrants our claiming a nobility for ourselves without an attendant rhetoric of alienation. There is something at best quaint, at worst self-delud-
ing, about this claim, since we are more likely now to desire simple
survival rather than nobility. Yet few of us, I suspect, escape dramas of
self-reflection where we try to distinguish those assertions about ourselves in which we can take pride from those that end in self-parody.
Abstraction becomes the necessary means to nobility when all our more
explicit forms of self-representation produce more parody than persuasion. For abstraction does not depend on narrative contexts and received
values. It offers the actions presented as approximating self-explanatory
displays, and it thereby posits the possibility (to be tested on each occasion) of something deeply enough embedded in our lives and our metaphors to take form despite the demise of particular beliefs. In effect,
abstraction gives even lovers of truth "enclosures of hypotheses,"[4] offering a recourse from what happens to each of their beloved propositions.

The work isolates qualities of the quest from the contingencies that determine its results.[5]

III

One cannot defend Stevens' ideas as ideas without denying the paradox on which they are founded – that their value as ideas is not in their truth claims per se but in the life they create within the scene that displays them. My account so far must therefore be treated as a pre-text for those most intense displays of imaginative power we call poems. If Stevens' prose is useful, it requires the critic to show how poetry makes the very difference Stevens names. But making this difference resonant is not an easy task. It requires an initial digression into Modernist painting, so that we can understand the instruments for using abstraction with which Stevens had to work. This is not to say that Stevens derived his principles from painterly examples. He was no doubt familiar with those examples and the ideology sustaining them, but familiarity need not entail influence; and concerns for influence may lead us astray. What matters is Stevens' sharing the artists' sense of the limits of representation and their desire to locate nobility in conditions of artistic action that can in some way become direct testimony to what they assert, thereby evading the ideologies of given social groups. As we pursue the resulting parallels we will see that ultimately Stevens wants to pose poetic language as a form of abstraction more resonant and representative than anything produced for the eye.

Mondrian is the most articulate spokesman for principles common in Stevens' New York art world and elaborated earlier in his friend Walter Pach's *The Masters of Modern Art* (1924):

> Art has shown that universal expression can only be created by a *real equation of the universal and the individual.* . . . Through intensification one creates successively on more profound planes; extension remains always on the same plane. Intensification be it noted is diametrically opposed to extension; they are at right angles to each other as are length and depth. . . . Art makes us realize that there are *fixed laws which govern and point to the use of the constructive elements of the composition and of the inherent interrelationships between them.* These laws may be regarded as subsidiary laws to the *fundamental* law of dynamic equivalence which creates *dynamic equilibrium and reveals the true content of reality.* . . . Real life is the *mutual interaction of two oppositions of the same value but of a different aspect of nature.* . . . We are now at the turning

point of this culture: the culture of particular form is approaching its end. The culture of determined relations has begun. . . . Non-figurative art demands . . . the *destruction* of particular form and the *construction* of a rhythm of mutual relations, of mutual forms or free lines. . . . It is of the greatest importance to note the destructive–constructive quality of dynamic equilibrium. . . . [This law] gives use to a number of different laws which . . . determine the manner in which dynamic equilibrium is achieved. The relations of position and those of dimension both have their own laws.[6]

Abstraction provides spiritual truth because it integrates two basic aspects of the pictorial surface. Let us call the first the "situating dimension," by which abstraction offers the mind something like purely conceptual realities not easily reducible to historical positivities. Insofar as we can call the work's "content" either the shapes and colors or the visual relations those elements create, we must acknowledge its capacity to render conditions so general that one cannot locate in the painting a specific ideology (although its rationale may be ideological). Yet the experience clearly carries a sense of significance. As Walter Pach put it, the pictorial plane affords "principles which are invariable for all men." Thus there is an odd but inescapable justice to Mondrian's claim "to represent balanced relations with ever greater exactness," offering "the purest representation of universality, of the harmony and unity which are inherent characteristics of the mind."[7]

Pure representations of the mind, however, would be only extensions, static illustrations of the new allegorical style called for by Wilhelm Worringer. The difference between that and Mondrian's stunning monumental qualities derives from a second dimension dictating how the abstract relations can be used. Let us call this the "presentational dimension," basing the distinction on the difference between what works represent or depict and what they can be said to display as the life created in the scene the work composes. Here relations become actual forces, giving testimony to the artist's assertions about the laws he represents as his content. What we see implicates how we see, so that the action of viewing becomes a process of intensification that literally connects universal features of the physical world with inescapable movements for the attentive mind. As we let our eye move around a Mondrian, we engage in a vital interchange between physical and self-reflexive properties. This is intensification, a literal condition of experience allowing the mind to recognize the ways in which its own powers are tied to the universal relations here given concrete form. Compositional acts by painter and viewer become dramatic realizations of a dynamic equilibrium – significant semantically without the metaphoric detour of particular scenic illusions or thematic arguments. Painting approaches the mystical without positing anything other than the concrete experience of that which is simply manifest in and as the painting. One can ignore the force of the work, but one cannot easily misinterpret it.

Stevens' reactions to such typical rhetoric of Modernist abstraction are characteristic. He sees precisely what is at stake: "It is easy to like Klee and Kandinsky. What is difficult is to like the many minor figures who do not communicate any theory that validates what they do and, in consequence, impress one as being without validity."[8] In other words, without an implicit theoretical concern or ideal for which the work is testimony, there is nothing for the presentational features to testify to or for; there are only visual relations without spiritual force. With a theoretical context, on the other hand, Stevens will recognize a painter like Marcel Gromaire presenting "the human spirit seeking its own architecture, its own *'mesure'* that will enable it to be in harmony with the world" (OP 291). But because his own medium is words, Stevens is extremely wary of the ways in which the painter's theories can distort "the intensity, the passion, of this search" (OP 291). Paradoxically, this need to make suspicion part of the process of securing idealizations warrants a claim that poetry is our richest form of abstract presentational testimony, since it can maintain the difference between specific beliefs and self-reflection on our desires for or capacity to believe:

> The theory of poetry, that is to say the total of the theories of poetry, often seems to become in time a mystical theology or, more simply, a mystique. . . . the reason is the same reason why the pictures in a museum of modern art often seem to become in time a mystical aesthetic, a prodigious search of appearance, as if to find a way of saying and of establishing that all things, whether below or above appearance, are one, and it is only through reality, in which they are reflected or, it may be, joined together, that we can reach them. Under such stress, reality changes from substance to subtlety. . . . Contending that this [quotations on the real from Cézanne and from Klee] sounds a bit like sacerdotal jargon, that is not too much to allow to those that have helped to create a new reality, a modern reality, since what has been created is nothing less. This reality is, also, the momentous world of poetry . . . Modern reality is a reality of decreation in which our revelations are not the revelations of belief, but the precious portents of our own powers. The great-

est truth that we could hope to discover . . . is that man's truth
is the final resolution of everything. (NA 173–75)

Prose can do no more. Indeed it has already done too much by giving
us terms like decreation and slogans like "man's truth," which either lead
us back to irony or make us wonder if Stevens is so banal that he ought
not be allowed to lead us at all. We must shift now to a passage of poetry
in order to see how the two dimensions of abstraction we have been
considering can give significance and bite to what prose all too easily and
perhaps superficially generates. In the process we must also explain how
a poet with as conservative a surface as Stevens can claim to be engaged
in a Modernist enterprise analogous to that of the painters. Let us begin
with one of his earliest poetic renderings of the abstractionist project,
near the close of "Examination of the Hero in a Time of War":

> It is not an image. It is a feeling.
> There is no image of the hero.
> There is a feeling as definition.
> How could there be an image, an outline,
> A design, a marble soiled by pigeons?
> The hero is a feeling, a man seen
> As if the eye was an emotion,
> As if in seeing we saw our feeling
> In the object seen and saved that mystic
> Against the sight, the penetrating
> Pure eye. Instead of allegory,
> We have and are the man, capable
> Of his brave quickenings, the human
> Accelerations that seem inhuman.   (CP 278–79)

Decreative energy here turns against standard ideals of the hero in order
to open a new, modern site where what matters is glimpsed mainly through
the effort to get clear of excess ideological baggage while still taking the
old journeys. Decreation so positions the imagination that it can discard
soiled metaphors while locating actual sources for the metaphors in the
literal testimony provided by the poem's specific course of reflections.
The ideal of heroism depends on the portents of our powers that the
poem itself generates.

In this fragment we glimpse some of the basic strategies Stevens elaborates for that task and the basic obstacles to it. The challenge, common
to all abstract art, is the danger of losing the man to the allegory. In
rejecting the dramatic rendering of individuals, the artist retains only
codified signs bound to fixed conceptual structures. Then, as Paul de

Man ceaselessly delighted in showing, the work's actual presentation undoes in time what allegory tries to compose in timeless space. But it may be possible to make what unfolds in time itself carry the allegorical weight. For it may be precisely in the qualities of that unfolding that there appear portents of a human presence not bound to doctrinal names for the hero. It may be in time that feelings take on a power capable of resisting names and even of participating in "brave quickenings" leading to the sublime threshold where the collapse of images lets the human verge on elemental inhuman powers.

These are large "ifs," but at the very least they clarify the demands Stevens puts on his language as a presentational force seeking to make vital in words what visual relations do for the monumental in painting. Here the syntax goes a long way toward realizing his claims by the "brave quickening" it produces. Simple introductory statements gradually expand into complex self-referring statements, so that the blend of syntax and complex aural play actually composes feeling without what would be the distortion of images. Ultimately the movement prepares a resonant return to plain statement, marked now by a reversal that measures our capacities to manipulate negation and contrast. The opening negations of the stanza set feelings against images. The final one sets allegory against the man as a means of showing that feelings can also produce confident assertions. Thus this final negation at once affirms the compositional force of decreation and indicates how that force leads well beyond the unmakings of infinite irony.

What Stevens has wrought here gets named most fully in the climax to the "It Must be Abstract" section of *Notes toward a Supreme Fiction,* where he gives his richest figure for this subsuming of allegory into the man we glimpse in our reading:

> The major abstraction is the idea of man
> And major man is its exponent, abler
> In the abstract than in his singular,
>
> More fecund as principle than particle . . .
> In being more than an exception, part
>
> Though an heroic part of the commonal. . . .
>
> It is of him, ephebe, to make, to confect
> The final elegance, not to console
> Nor sanctify, but plainly to propound.   (CP 388–89)

Major man as "exponent" is a remarkable conception of how time can become a presentational factor in reading. The exponent is an interpreter or interpretive sign, but its mathematical overtones cast interpreting as a form of power, a way of multiplying the energies invoked by a factor that repeats the phenomenon in intensified form. The exponent is the quickening created by the figures that language composes as it presents its claims. Presentational force articulates a concrete hero and projects through him the abstract content of a figure who carries the allegorical burden as a modern Everyman. In defining such principles, poetic speech becomes part of the commonal, part of the very theater which replaces an old representational stage and allows the artist to act out feelings an audience grasps "as of two emotions becoming one" (CP 329–40). This abstract scope of exponential activity so incorporates an artificial elegance into the processes of syntax that the poem can plainly propound the very ideas that its language acts out. Concrete testimony need not depend on dramatic illusions, or on disguised thematics, or on covert intentions framing a narrative (all the sources of allegory), because the language itself can take responsibility for what it asserts. And the quickening of language can carry the burden otherwise put on metaphoric indirectness, so it makes sense to think that so intense an expressive medium can be devoted to plain propoundings.

IV

To discuss the role of painterly parallels in Stevens is necessarily to confront the presence of two poets – one a sensualist epicure, perhaps closest to the Fauves, and the other an epicure's reflective mind working at the limits of sensation. I compare early Stevens and the Fauves because they managed to blend Impressionist and Postimpressionist elements without invoking the expressionist psychological melodramas that one finds in other branches of Postimpressionism. Instead, the Fauves made the brush stroke a form of exuberant materialism, which Stevens parallels thematically and stylistically in poems like "Sea Surface Full of Clouds" and "Six Significant Landscapes." In such poems, painterly emphases on the composition of visual relations and atmospheric properties become the basis for a radical critique of humanism. If "the soil is man's intelligence" (CP 36), then its fullest artistic realization is not in the displacements brought by ideas but in the capacity to suffuse what in the flesh is immortal with a consciousness become virtually a part of the weather. "I am what is around me" (CP 86) – not the interpreter of the scene but an instrument for rendering anew, in an aural medium, an atmosphere that intensifies the scene's sensual effects and shows the spirit how fully it can live a physical life. Abstraction is, like philosophy, the horny breath of the elders. Poetry is, on the other hand, not Susannah's masturbatory fullness but Quince's improvisational elegance as he composes the scene into musically rendered sensual forces.

This Stevens we shall not study here. Michel Benamou and others have outlined the basic concerns, and a full analysis would take us very far astray.[9] Our attention must be focused on the second Stevens, the one who makes this sensualist his dramatic contrast. This Stevens, devoted to abstraction, still distrusts thematic interpretation and still seeks versions of Symbolist "atmosphere." But, like Mondrian's, his new atmosphere has little to do with visual appearances or the play of artifice composing an alternative physical space. What it will require first emerges clearly in two basic features of "The Idea of Order at Key West." The solipsist speaker of *Harmonium* seeks a "we," wherein he can share a world with Ramon Fernandez and with the singer. That requires turning away from the sensations offered by a scene in order to concentrate on how the sensations are framed. The form of "we" depends on shareable structures for processing and assessing information. Second, the basic process becomes an act of interpretation; what matters is how the scene leads one to reflect. Just as the early poetry defines a model of agency attuned to the unfolding of scenes or metaphors, the new poetry must locate "you as you are" by learning to "throw away the lights, the definitions, / and say of what you see in the dark / That it is this or that it is that" (CP 183). Destroying reference (CP 279) allows one to refuse the rotted names and concentrate on the form of our knowings:

> Nothing must stand
> Between you and the shapes you take
> When the crust of shape has been destroyed.   (CP 183)

How this production of shapes in the decreation of the crust of shape constitutes poetry of the highest order is perhaps clearest if we trace a sequence of three poems devoted to freeing abstraction from the claims of perception, so that it resides ultimately in the display of powers immediately available in the activity of reading: "A Study of Two Pears," "Someone Puts a Pineapple Together," and "The Pastor Caballero."

My first example offers us the Stevens of the first section of *Parts of a World*. War, time, and self-consciousness about the limits of ironic self-consciousness have made it impossible to speak either of sensuous plenitude or of dreams of order. These subjects leave out too much of the world. "Salvation here?" (CP 191), the opening poem of the volume asks, then answers that any possibility of salvation requires coming to terms with a life that is "faster than any scene." The world can be put together, but not with our hands (CP 192). The need then is for a new kind of hero, for new powers that it becomes the task of "A Study of Two Pears" to spell out:

I

Opusculum paedagogum.
The pears are not viols,
Nudes or bottles.
They resemble nothing else.

II

They are yellow forms
Composed of curves
Bulging toward the base.
They are touched red.

III

They are not flat surfaces
Having curved outlines.
They are round
Tapering toward the top.

IV

In the way they are modelled
There are bits of blue.
A hard dry leaf hangs
From the stem.

V

The yellow glistens.
It glistens with various yellows,
Citrons, oranges and greens
Flowering over the skin.

VI

The shadows of the pears
Are blobs on the green cloth.
The pears are not seen
As the observer wills.

The title establishes the new space abstraction must explore, a site between art and perception, while also suggesting the basic problem that such exploration must face. I take it that the "study" refers to a painting, which in turn affords us an opportunity to study how we go about seeing in a vital way. Yet the very framework of the study may eventually prove as limiting and self-mocking as the Latin pedagogy that sets the scene. For as we become aware of how our attention becomes vital, we may feel trapped by the frames that reward its visual orientation. Two negations begin the reflective processes – the first proposing a practical context at odds with the visual vitality, the second adapting for vision a version of Spinoza's "every determination is a negation." The negative frame then makes possible something like a Cézannian process of realization. Words treated virtually as brush strokes compose visual details of the "study," which in turn lead us to piece together a pear as if the object were freshly before us, seen for the first time. Realization represents, but what is represented is not a world of ordinary objects and conventionalized vision. Indeed, once the process begins it soon exceeds the object eliciting it. So in the central stanzas we move from specific negations and sharpened attention to what must be taken as purposive aspects of appearance. We think of a modelling will.[10] But then the will quickly leads to grounds beyond the subjective maker through Stevens' remarkably inventive use of the clichéd metaphor "flowering." As perception becomes active, and especially as it comes to recognize a dynamic principle at work in eliciting its activity, straightforward names must yield to metaphor if they are to be at all adequate to the situation. Stated this baldly, however, we find ourselves making an observation which would hold true of any intense situation. Stevens' specific metaphor complicates matters considerably. Up to this point the poem had relied on a presentational movement but had not sought an abstract situating – quite the contrary. Now the action shifts from seeing to reflecting upon one's seeing. As the pear becomes most fully itself before the eye, it must become something else: the fruit must act as a flower does if the mind is to appreciate fully its appearance as a fruit. Then, as flowering seems to capture the particular act of emergence, we recognize that the term applies to a good deal more than the pear. The flowering is also a process of the mind's own blossoming within a world formerly perceived only from a distance. The painting brush, the writer's recasting, and the observer's attention all here flower, suggesting that when mind too becomes fully itself it must at the same time become other, must take on an identity that no perception qua perception can register. Perception at its most intense requires our entering the order of metaphor, requires the intensification of art. This indeed is why we need a painting to learn how to see a pear.

Williams would conclude the poem at this point. Stevens adds a highly enigmatic stanza that brings further dimensions to the processes we have been considering. If "pears are not seen / as the observer wills," then we probably should understand the moments of the mind's flowering as its reward for not willing. This emergent metaphor, as opposed to an alle-

gorically imposed one, suggests that the mind can exceed itself by disci-
plining itself to the spare style and emphatically simple architecture that
aligns it to what it names, just as painting flowers in a Cézannian realization. Attention is the route to transformation, ultimately exploding
even clichéd metaphor into a strange equivalence between what colors
do and what minds do – that is, flower to become more fully themselves.
If we stop here, however, we have not interpreted the negative movement of the last stanza or understood the pressure that such states exerted
upon Stevens to develop a fuller abstract mode. The mind is not like
pears; it is not fully itself in its flowering because it proceeds to transform
the shadows into a very different kind of overdetermined language, the
blobs on the green cloth.[11] The shadows of the pears are perceptually
part of the scene, and could be part of the flowering (as in Picasso's 1908
still life). But as "blobs" the shadows lead beyond the scene by taking
on the traditional symbolic overtones that make shadows suggest a ter-
rifying otherness. Physical shadows then become metaphorical shadows,
which then become metapoetic shadows serving as an emblem for the
very overdetermined absence language is in the process of creating. Thus
the final expression returns to negations, but this time in the passive
voice because this "not" no longer determines a perceptual scene but
marks an absolute boundary between presence and absence.

At stake is not what one sees but whether one sees at all (in the strong
sense of "sees"). There are two possible blocks. "As the observer wills"
can refer either to a temporal state (observing cannot take place at the
same time as willing) or to a modal state (observing cannot be brought
into accord with the dictates of will). In either case, the *as* marks the deep
problem. Observing requires an equivalence of willing and seeing, of
individual needs and transparent disclosures, which is impossible for the
kind of creature that sees itself seeing pears as flowering. Metaphors seem
triumphs of attention as they emerge, but as we reflect on the emerging
they lead also to our recognition that shadows are a good deal more than
physical phenomena. A self that can flower cannot escape moments when
its percepts become shadows of a displaced or "monstrous" humanness.
As one wills, one encounters the absolute negative, the law of human
differences by which the *as* of metaphor seems to entail the *as* of willed
impositions on the real.

Much of Stevens' subsequent work is devoted to negating the negation
in "the pears are not seen as the observer wills." If the statement is true,
perhaps there is something positive in the difference, perhaps poetry can
shift from "substance to subtlety" by treating the many forms of "as the
observer wills" so that they become themselves a plausible reality, "As if
in seeing we saw our feeling / In the object seen and saved that mystic

/ Against the sight" (CP 278–79). Here perhaps is where the man steps forth from the allegory and takes a heroic part in the commonal.

These possibilities form the context and specific subject of my second example, "Someone Puts a Pineapple Together." While the poem is too long and intricate for a thorough reading here, the relevant materials are fairly easy to state briefly. We need attend first to the context of the poem. Stevens never collected it, publishing it instead as the second of "Three Academic Pieces" in *The Necessary Angel*. Whereas "A Study of Two Pears" took its place in a section of a book mapping the problems in Stevens' earlier position on fictions, this poem appears as part of a reconsideration of the theory of metaphor seeking to posit satisfying relations between the *as* of seeing and the *as* of willing. The subject of these academic pieces is how poetry can be said to handle resemblance so that it can stand as itself resembling the real. How can the energies poetry focuses not displace the real but attach the mind to it, thereby projecting the will as the basic instrument allowing realities to emerge? If "the pro-liferation of resemblances extends an object" (NA 78), then poetry's "intensification of reality by resemblance increases realization":

> It is as if a man who lived indoors should go outdoors on a day of sympathetic weather. His realization of the weather would exceed that of a man who lives outdoors. It might, in fact, be intense enough to convert the real world about him into an imagined world. In short a sense of reality keen enough to be in excess of the normal sense of reality creates a reality of its own. Here what matters is that the intensification of the sense of real-ity create a resemblance: that reality of its own is a reality. (NA 78–79)

The domestic creates a threshold for the sublime because it makes available resemblances (including contrasts) which allow us to intensify our response to particulars and then to abstract our powers of intensifi-cation as themselves elements of a reality. Within this dialectic, poetry serves the ultimately narcissistic role of keeping our images of the human as part of the real. (NA 80) Even though we constantly outlive the spe-cific ideals this narcissism generates, our irreducible will to use such facts as principles of resemblance, or measures of a spiritual weather, keeps the ideal "alive with an enormous life" (NA 82). It is as if the reality of poetry realized an *as* that captures a necessary interconnection between observing and willing. That interconnection constitutes the immanent life of value, whose theory is the theory of poetry.

"Someone Puts a Pineapple Together" (NA 83–89) celebrates the irreducible union that makes these two principles a basis for the entire process of idealization. The poem need not rely on analogies to painting, because it is after larger resemblances, after a sense of artifice at the very core of seeing where self and world form something like Whitehead's prehensive event: "He sees it in this tangent of himself. / And in this tangent it becomes a thing / Of weight on which the weightless rests." Given that union, one can move from the specific tangents defined by metaphors to the nature of metaphor itself. Metaphor distorts seeing. But it is also the only power we have sufficient to resist these distortions and restore a sense of the mind's place as the valuing principle embedded in sight. In defying "the metaphor that murders metaphor," the observer alive with artifice "seeks as image a second of the self / . . . the particular tingle in a proclamation / that makes it say the little things it says." This "second of the self" defines what abstraction contributes to the event. We experience a moment of presence in which the *as* of willing makes observing valuable, produces a simulacrum of the real capable of serving as an aide in a mock-heroic epistemological duel, and gives the self ideal projections of its own possibilities. So the poem can conclude in celebration of precisely that reality within the real that the prose had simply hypothesized as a plausible "second" to perception. The pineapple becomes

> An object, the sum of its complications, seen
> And unseen. This is everybody's world.
> Here the total artifice reveals itself
>
> As the total reality. . . .
>   It is that which is distilled
> In the prolific ellipses that we know,
>
> In the planes that tilt hard revelations on
> The eye, a geometric glitter, tiltings
> As of sections collecting toward the greenest cone.

Each of the poems we have examined opens possible lines of imaginative reflection. It would thus be silly to insist on a developmental dialectic foreign to Stevens' interest in multiple frames for the world. Nonetheless there are developments in Stevens' career – if not resolutions to contradictions, then at least the elaboration of new possibilities with different configurations, limits, and modes of self-comprehension. My third example, "The Pastor Caballero," defines one of these possibilities not available within the essentially perceptual situations of the previous poems. Here, as Wordsworth does in his "Elegiac Stanzas," Stevens takes as his basic subject not acts of perception but painterly interpretations of experience. This provides access to productive dimensions of the will to metaphor not available to interpretive logics based upon perceptual schema. We move in effect from the epistemological effects of metaphor to the psychological powers of metaphor makers, somewhat as Picasso shifts from the still lifes of analytic Cubism to the playful synthetic work that freed him for major canvases like *Three Musicians,* which he painted in the early twenties. In Stevens' case, the poem provides a painterly analogue for producing metaphors and serves as a transition between *Transport to Summer* and the programmatic summary on abstraction constituting the first part of *Notes toward a Supreme Fiction.*

"The Pastor Caballero" is one of those odd, minor Stevens poems that seem initially awkward and flat but that under careful scrutiny flower into an intricately intelligent statement:

> The importance of its hat to a form becomes
> More definite. The sweeping brim of the hat
> Makes of the form Most Merciful Capitan,
>
> If the observer says so: grandiloquent
> Locution of a hand in a rhapsody.
> Its line moves quickly with the genius
>
> Of its improvisation until, at length,
> It enfolds the head in a vital ambiance,
> A vital, linear ambiance. The flare
>
> In the sweeping brim becomes the origin
> Of a human evocation, so disclosed
> That, nameless, it creates an affectionate name,
>
> Derived from adjectives of deepest mine.
> The actual form bears outwardly this grace,
> An image of the mind, an inward mate.
>
> Tall and unfretted, a figure meant to bear
> Its poisoned laurels in this poisoned wood,
> High in the height that is our total height.
>
> The formidable helmet is nothing now.
> These two go well together, the sinuous brim
> And the green flauntings of the hours of peace.   (CP 379)

I do not know any specific painting to which this poem alludes. I suspect, in fact, that anything more than suggestion of resemblance would weaken the assertion of power Stevens presents. For the important thing is not how poems, or paintings, refer to sources but what they lead us to think and feel about ourselves. Notice how the poem's opening even refuses all questions of scene and setting in order to emphasize questions of how artifacts produce significance. It is not names, but acts and means of naming, that demand attention, primarily because only on that level can one hope to resist the tendency of names to become contaminated rhetorical gestures. This poem about heroism and nobility testifies to what it asserts by foregrounding the powers of abstraction to generate those very values without relying on myth or dogma. Names are derived from direct projections of human desire. The artist's acts display principles and passions expressing the constant source of our names and providing values for their referents.

Such abstract situating puts a direct burden on the presentational level of the poem. It is here that the poetic line must earn for poetry the right to compare itself to painting by dramatizing poetry's capacity as a portent of powers. In effect, this makes the real portrait here a clarification of what poetry can portray. Stevens' first vehicle for this is his control of the sentence unit, the linguistic correlate of the painter's "hand in rhapsody." In developing the poem's claims about forms, the sentence units become increasingly complicated as they prepare for the heroic rhetoric of the sixth stanza. This is not merely a matter of syntax. Stevens brilliantly plays sentences against stanzaic units so that until the sixth stanza the sentences create a "vital linear ambiance" overflowing the verse boundaries. The effect is most impressive in the fourth, pivotal stanza because that is the only stanza without a completed sentence. At the poem's center, the poet names the origin of art's names, but that act itself must be suspended, must resist closure because the names involved derive not from any resting place in reference but rather depend on what is itself suspended within the filigree of language.

Foregrounded syntactic control is then supplemented by semantic and structural effects. The poem consists of two basic segments, an initial description of the way the hat comprises a fully expressive artistic gesture and the synethetic, self-reflexive commentary of the last two sentences. These sentences in effect try to make explicit the import of the poem. But they do so less as statement than as a literal embodiment of the space of mind which reflection makes available as one comes to recognize how the portrait embodies "adjectives of deepest mine" (and mind). Normally it would take allegory to give shadowy forms to these purported human potentials. Here the allegory is inseparable from the actual movement of the lines: The object rendered defines what the rendering accomplishes. We see the outward image become inward mate, and then we watch that equation sustain a somewhat overblown rhetoric because of the complex reference of the "figure" metaphor. The hero who can bear heroic names in the poisoned wood of history gains his power from his situation, from the fact that he exists as a figure uniting the artist's construct, the Pastor's image, and the viewer-reader's sense of contemplating in the external expression an image of her own inner life.

This triumphant assertion, with all its intelligence, nonetheless seems too shrill, too dogmatic, too much a matter of attributing traits to external rather than internal images. This is why Stevens needs a final stanza where a retrospective power earns the right to say whose woods these are and what claims they license. Instead of gestures outward, all the assertions are indexical and self-referential.[12] The helmet is "nothing now," both because it no longer signifies heroism and because the "now" has been so thickened by thought that it requires no specific object or name. Art creates a site where loss can be transformed into triumphant specificity. And now the flamboyant "flauntings" begin to make sense as a celebration of the power to name. Once the painting becomes our hero, what more appropriate gesture than to flaunt, especially to flaunt in the form of a second indexical, a synthetic "these" that celebrates the painterly, writerly, and readerly acts this simple poem offers. We even learn here that the apparently arbitrary figure of the poisoned woods had a probable basis in the green background of the painting. But we learn that only after the fact, only in this deliberate "collecting toward the greenest cone" that constitutes the space of art where we contemplate not objects but human gestures. Here even the oldest, most conventional of allegorical equations, that of green with peace, takes on precise, justified meanings in the literal testimony of the work. A green that can flaunt itself composes the very peace it asserts.

V

Flauntings in themselves, however, must be silent about the significance of the powers asserted. Stevens needs to elaborate supplementary contexts for clarifying what matters in what we experience so that he can project the connections that experience has to the practices and concerns basic to ordinary life. The following passage is so ambitious in that quest that it must be couched in elaborate self-mockery:

> A scholar, in his Segmenta, left a note,
> As follows, "The Ruler of Reality,
> If more unreal than New Haven, is not
>
> A real ruler, but rules what is unreal.
> In addition, there were draftings of him, thus:
> He is the consort of the Queen of Fact.
>
> . . . He is the theorist of life, not death,
> The total excellence of its total book. . . .

"This man abolishes by being himself
That which is not ourselves: the regalia,
The attributions, the plume and helmet-ho."

Again, "He has thought it out, he thinks it out,
As he has been and is and, with the Queen
Of Fact, lies at his ease beside the sea."

XXVIII

If it should be true that reality exists
In the mind . . .

. . . , it follows that
Real and Unreal are two in one: New Haven
Before and after one arrives or, say,

Bergamo on a postcard, Rome after dark,
Sweden described . . .

This endlessly elaborating poem
Displays the theory of poetry,
As the life of poetry. A more severe,

More harassing master would extemporize
Subtler, more urgent proof that the theory
Of poetry is the theory of life

As it is, in the intricate evasions of as,
In things seen and unseen, created from nothingness,
The heavens, the hells, the worlds, the longed-for-lands:
                                            (CP 485–86)

At the climax of "An Ordinary Evening in New Haven," Stevens makes the process of abstraction the basic vehicle by which the life of poetry displays what can become the elements of a theory of life. Two elements in particular will warrant the kind of philosophical support one can gather from thinkers like Wittgenstein – the site abstraction produces as a synthesis of the real and the unreal, and the way the *as* eventually becomes the concrete operator that most succinctly and clearly connects the syntax of art to a general theory of value. I envision these two factors as thematic extensions of the situational and presentational aspects of abstraction. The site abstraction creates substitutes for dramatic illusion this more fundamental play of ideal and denotative elements, while the *as* allows the presentational testimony of art to encompass the most basic human needs. Because "I have not but I am and as I am, I am" (CP 405), identity depends not on descriptions but on exponential indicators whose powers of magnification produce a dialectic of the real and unreal central to the possibility of there being distinctive human values. Thus by reflecting on the *as* we have a paradigm for how Modernist abstract concreteness becomes a testimony to powers; we locate a principle inviting comparison to Wittgenstein's exemplary modern philosophical enterprise; and we discover a readerly dynamic for treating the *as* as a ground for forms of nobility. Finally, we make plausible and useful a critical enterprise which Harry Berger called, with the idealized disdain for ideals that only a deconstructive historicist can muster, "as–kissing raised to the level of a humanistic ideal."

It behooves us to know the *as* we intend to kiss. For a poet the primary features are situational. The *as* is in essence the basic principle of metaphor, abstracted from the various particular vehicles soiled by history. At one pole it is the quintessence of flowering, because it is the term for equivalence in the present. We see *x* with the aspects of *y,* and thus make it possible to treat something as capable of satisfying the observer's emotional investment. Here the unreal, the projection of desire, consorts playfully with the Queen of Fact. At the other pole the *as* can be extremely general, enabling the poet to stand outside the aspectual dimensions of seeing so that he can describe them as such, can say that this may appear as a duck or as a rabbit depending upon certain conditions. He recognizes the place of Jamesian plurality, but from a perspective that addresses what all the acts share. The *as* positions the poet beyond the differences that perspectivism insists upon, yet allows him to show how the various attitudes might be available to everyone, "a visibility of thought, / in which hundreds of eyes, in one mind, see at once" (CP 488). For the one mind can see as each of those eyes might see, yet make its reflections on that sight available to all.

As we consider these forms of content, we also make obvious an even more significant aspect of the *as*. Because it is an equivalence term, what it asserts can easily become indistinguishable from the presentational testimony provided in how the assertions are rendered. The *as* literally produces resemblances, affords shifts in the level of discourse, and allows us to entertain provisional sympathies with a variety of attitudes. We see our seeing of *x* as *y*. Within such self-consciousness, the abstract *as* refers directly to the way poetry crosses life, because it names the state of equivalence basic to all acts of valuing. Reading becomes a paradigmatic form for such valuing: In the equivalences it provides we take on other identities and observe ourselves as we so dispose our wills. Poems establish possibilities of relation that readers take on as portents of their possible powers, as they read. Finally, poems concentrate attention upon the basic ontological property of the *as*. It need not be a derivational relationship, a way of interpreting what has independent status. Rather, because the *as* is an equivalence term, the fact that moments exist as some one thing or another means that unreal and real consort in the actuality of "event." (CP 476) There are no independent terms one can prize off the moment. Thus there are not worlds and interpretations, but worlds as interpreted in a variety of ways, each perhaps best articulated not by descriptions but by making manifest the energies involved:

> The poem is the cry of its occasion
> Part of the res itself and not about it.
> The poet speaks the poem as it is,
>
> Not as it was: part of the reverberation
> Of a windy night as it is, when the marble statues
> Are like newspapers blown by the wind. He speaks
>
> By sight and insight as they are.   (CP 473)

I stumble with this epistemology. Yet I must ask you to bear with me through one more intensifying of the abstraction before I show how all of this comes to fruition as a context for Wittgenstein's much less pretentious language (which, because of its lack of pretension, has been misread as a variant of behaviorism). Imagine stepping back from this sense of equivalences which I claim to be central to Stevens' understanding of values. Imagine how our lives as a whole appear in relation to our capacities to wield the intricacies of *as*. This is for Stevens the supreme fiction, supreme consort of fact in its real unreality. Its first incarnation takes place for the mountain Chocorua as it reflects on its place within a force capable of apprehending the physical world not simply as facts, but as values:

> Cloud-casual, metaphysical metaphor,
> But resting on me, thinking in my snow,
> Physical if the eye is quick enough,
> So that, where he was, there is an enkindling, where
> He is, the air changes and grows fresh to breathe.
>
> The air changes, creates and re-creates, like strength,
> And to breathe is a fulfilling of desire,
> A clearing, a detecting, a completing,
> A largeness lived and not conceived, a space
> That is an instant nature, brilliantly.   (CP 301)

By "An Ordinary Evening in New Haven," the focus on a physical element expands to include the "endlessly elaborating poem" of the world. What is physical is inseparable from a power which tries to imagine itself as a whole, even as it knows that by so doing it only proliferates itself. "Metaphysical metaphor" becomes the very capacity to register the ways the unreal makes the real become actual. Then, as we approach this maximum degree of abstraction, the process can reverse itself. The simplest acts, like arriving in New Haven or registering the weather, take place on a metaphysical stage. The theory of poetry – or better, poetry as theorizing – becomes the theory of life, because it puts within contemplative brackets the essential force that makes value possible, the interdependence of the unreal and the real. The *as* becomes a metaphysical emblem projecting the endlessly proliferating incarnations of the spirit in the flesh. The *as* provides a body for the giant within whom we think and from whom we feel at once a clearing and a completing of the very forms of desire.

VI

Hegel on substance and spirit, Sartre on *en-soi* and *pour-soi,* had developed similar visions. But for them the theory of life precluded poetry because the criteria for theory required explaining the unreal through an elaborate metaphysical machinery. It takes decreation, the modern form of Occam's razor, to make the life lived in a reflective mode like that of poetry a direct focusing on the ways values are established in life. Similarly, it takes Wittgenstein, an even greater proponent of a decreation that becomes a composing of desire, to make us grasp just how rich is Stevens' *as* as a mode for realizing the potential of Modernist abstraction. Two themes in particular bond these figures – the effort, basic in early Wittgenstein, to imagine how philosophy can think like Chocorua to specify the threshold where the condition of value enters the "real" world of facts; and the project, elaborated in Wittgenstein's last work, of locating within the *as* models of human agency incompatible with behaviorist reductionism (or, I might add, with the various historical quasi-determinisms that tempt contemporary critics). While I shall, all too briefly, use Wittgenstein to dignify Stevens, the reader will see the reciprocal effect whereby Stevens' concerns help us attend to connections within Wittgenstein all too rarely appreciated by philosophers.[13]

Wittgenstein's *Tractatus* articulates what would soon become the Vienna Circle's radical divorce between value and fact; or, in Stevens' terms, between the unreal and the real:

6.41   The sense of the world must lie outside the world. In the world everything is as it is, and everything happens as it does happen: *in* it no value exists – and if it did, it would have no value. If there is any value that does have value, it must lie outside the whole sphere of what happens and is the case. For all that happens and is the case is accidental. . . .

6.42   And so it is impossible for there to be propositions of ethics. Propositions can express nothing of what is higher.

6.43   It is clear that ethics cannot be put into words. Ethics is transcendental. (Ethics and aesthetics are one and the same.)[14]

The logic here makes powerful use of Kantian themes. First, what can be named must be a fact in the world. Names mean because they have referents; otherwise they are senseless. Then, as Kant argued, the condition determining the world *as it is* must be the working of empirical laws, those regularities within which concepts like freedom and value make no sense. The world is lawful, but its laws are "accidental" because there is no reason they could not be otherwise; they simply are the case with no appeal to purposes and justifications.

But Wittgenstein did not come only as the precursor of Positivism. He cares so much about what the world denies because he wants to understand, as Kant did, where one can locate the sphere of values so that one can still propose ways philosophical thought might make a difference in the theory of life. For early Wittgenstein that difference is primarily negative or decreative. Again restating Kant, Wittgenstein thought that philosophy could clarify the nature of value only by denying adherents to analytic methods any access to it. Value is the antithesis of propositional statement because values (in the strong sense) cannot be accidental. Values depend on ends and purposes, even if our only access to them can take the form of accepting our accidental destinies. Recognizing what philosophy cannot do, we might use that limit to imagine alternative relations to a world within which the unreal can play a cogent part. Attention to natural laws keeps us within the world; the life of values requires our occupying positions from which we can frame the accidental and take up attitudes towards it *as* a whole. We must judge from a position not within space and time but at the border that these conditions of perception impose. Thus ethics and aesthetics become one, because both spheres involve the kind of viewing in which the mind tries to frame a situation and take a stance toward it as a whole. So conceived, both the aesthetic and the ethical border on the theological, allowing us to see ourselves in the same way that Chocorua reflects on what contains it: "To view the world *sub specie aeterni* is to view it as a whole – a limited

whole. Feeling the world as a limited whole – it is this that is mystical."
(TLP 6.45) And in this sense of the mystical we recognize the need for a
model of agency that cannot be represented by any form of rational or
perspectival thought. The self that occupies these margins can only be
described by the life that is lived in the scenes that it composes:

> Ethics does not treat of the world, Ethics must be a condition of
> the world, like logic. Ethics and aesthetics are one. . . . (N 77)
> As the subject is not a part of the world but a presupposition of
> its existence, so good and evil are predicates of the subject, not
> properties in the world . . . (N 79) Where in the world is a meta-
> physical subject to be found? You say that it is just as it is for the
> eye and the visual field. But you do not actually see the eye. And
> I think that nothing in the visual field would enable one to infer
> that it is seen from an eye. The thinking subject is surely mere
> illusion. But the willing subject exists. If the will did not exist,
> neither would there be that centre of the world, which we call
> the "I," and which is the bearer of ethics. What is good and evil
> is essentially the I, not the world; the "I," the "I" is what is
> deeply mysterious. The "I" is not an object. (N 80)

This nonobjective "I" – at once too deep for words and too private to
be manifest except in the universal function of each willing subject pursuing its differences – could serve as the typical speaker of a late Stevens
poem. We need abstraction for the qualities of will to manifest themselves; and we need a concept of the unreal in order to specify the kind
of life that can be lived at the margin of facts, at once seeking difference
and desiring their consort. But if we remain within analogies to the early
Wittgenstein we never get past the condition of Chocorua, the immobile
contemplator of the force the unreal gives our contemplative lives. Late
Stevens, like late Wittgenstein, adds a principle for extending the life of
the deep subject into the flux of the quotidian. Then both the poet and
the philosopher can at once disclose the marginal nature of the willing
subject and get beyond contemplation to a sense of how the unreal per-
meates ordinary life. Both ethics and aesthetics become more than abstract
statements about values, and the theory of poetry becomes the basis for
a full theory of life.

The similarities between the two thinkers' late work most clearly come
into focus when Wittgenstein too turns to the *as* as his emblem for certain
powers of mind manifest only in its most elemental processes. Recall the
first *as* we saw him employ: "In the world everything is *as* it is, and
everything happens *as* it does happen." The *as* here is an empiricist one,
maintained by a subject attempting to separate observation from will,

being from persons. The *as* is simply an operator that marks a congruence or equivalence between names and facts. The *as* projects no resemblances and thus brings no qualities to the occasion.

By section eleven of *Philosophical Investigations,* however, radical changes have occurred. The section begins with two competing models of seeing the world – one in which the *as* remains a copying operation, the other in which the concept of likeness replaces that of the copy. In the latter case we see an object "as we interpret it" (PI 193), so the philosopher's task is to fill out the grammar of this *as* by analyzing the many different dimensions of psychic life that contribute to this interpretive process. Now the *as* produces a constant tension between the real and the unreal, condensing into a drop of grammar a great deal of the fustian regarding connections between the theory of poetry and the theory of life proposed by Idealist thinkers from Hegel to Heidegger. We need simply reflect on the ways in which our manipulating the *as* establishes powers within ordinary experience that flesh out what Wittgenstein had attributed to the deep subject confined at the margins of the real. And once we see how such elemental functions become testimony to substantial philosophical distinctions, we should recognize the price we pay if we translate Stevens back into the pure thematics of Idealist critics or their materialist opponents. We see that what matters is precisely an abstracting power sufficient to allow the most concrete linguistic elements to carry philosophical weight in their own right. Wittgenstein and Stevens both elaborate a Modernist imperative whose quest for concreteness as a philosophical tool leads ultimately to locating an "indefiniteness" at the core of human experience and then putting it "correctly and unfalsified, into words" (PI 227). The theorizing of poetry becomes the theory of life by positing alternatives for both empiricist reductionism and Idealist ontologizing. The being of beings is simply a matter of how the I manipulates "the intricate evasions of as."

VII

As Wittgenstein's Modernist adaptations of Idealist ontology to ordinary experience clarify Stevens on the weaving of the unreal into our cultural habits, Stevens plays the equally important role of casting this ontology so that we see it framing our experience of the world as a whole. The poet's aspects extend our perceptions, putting the indefiniteness Wittgenstein tried to specify in relation to the speculative ambitions and expansive investments of the lyrical mind. The philosopher purifies language, enabling the poet's fictions to serve as plausible expressive features of a modern reality. For Stevens poetry most fully epitomizes its philosophical roles as an abstracting power when it turns self-reflexively on the processes of reading. That action necessarily unites what poems can describe and what they must enact, so attention to reading becomes our access to the site of abstraction and the means by which we test on our own pulses the possibly transpersonal dimensions of the exponential *as*. It is as readers that we locate adjectives of deepest mine and recognize what and how we share the processes of fit and of intensification a poem describes. These identifications then bring into play the second, presentational aspect of abstraction because they afford literal testimony to how as we entertain the "as" we become figures of desire participating in the life of major man. The reading motif allows Stevens the plain propoundings of his last poems because it shifts the burden of lyricism from the confections of metaphor to the simple, self-reflexive process of aligning ourselves to the unfoldings of a speech anyone can speak. Reading focuses the indefiniteness which personal desire keeps at the center of plain propoundings, so that these propoundings serve also as "portents of our own powers," in much the same way as the activities of viewing are necessary to produce the intensifications that Mondrian elaborates. As we watch ourselves read about our reading the theory of poetry is necessarily the theory of life.

Once again it takes poetry to show how these are not mere pieties. Or, I might say, it takes the testimony of reading to show that what seem pieties for the critic become justified by the investments to which they give expression in a work of art. Let us therefore turn to Stevens' "Large Red Man Reading," a poem about completing the physiognomy of earth. The conclusion asks us to see an unreal, giant reader as he is read by those "who would have wept to step barefoot into reality" (whether the weeping is for joy or fear, we are not told):

> That would have wept and been happy, have shivered in the
>   frost
> And cried out to feel it again, have run fingers over leaves
> And against the most coiled thorn, have seized on what was
>   ugly
>
> And laughed, as he sat there reading, from out of the purple
>   tabulae
> The outlines of being and its expressings, the syllables of its
>   law:
> Poesis, poesis, the literal characters, the vatic lines,
>
> Which in those ears and in those thin, those spended hearts,
> Took on color, took on shape and the size of things as they are

And spoke the feeling for them, which was what they had
    lacked.   (CP 424)

The content one reads has significance primarily for the processes it sus-
tains and the mediations these allow between Chocorua's giant and those
he represents. Reading, then, becomes a powerful alternative to what
lovers of truth seek, because it shifts the burden of language from representation to representativeness, from objective statements to poten-
tially transpersonal functions. This occurs in two registers that are con-
joined in the brilliant union of subjective and objective forces Stevens
puts to work in his conclusion's rendering of the *as*. The giant speaks the
feeling for "things as they are," in Wittgenstein's empiricist sense. Yet
he also speaks for things as they can enter feelings and thus stands for the
constitutive power of analogical relations, as real as any empirical
description.

Many poets have made similar claims. Stevens adds to those a
remarkable level of self-reference – not of the poet to his own act, but of
the reader directed to use his experience as the concrete evidence for the
poem's claims. In reading, one becomes the giant; one no longer needs
the testimony of Chocorua. First, reading participates in his constitutive
speech because it requires our taking up the aspects that the poem's words
offer. As we read, we can reflect on ourselves trying out possibilities,
experiencing it this way or that, until particulars cohere and the text is
seen in the size or scope of things it can maintain. Poems need not establish true descriptions. They instead establish the power of language to
make visible aspects of the world. In reading the poem it is the "characters of being" that are said to come alive. And as we read we test that
claim by proposing certain fits or alignments by which we speak a feeling
our world otherwise would lack. Reading can be literally the presence of
that aspect-consciousness allowing us to say "now I see" or "seen like
this it does makes sense to believe I possess certain powers."

But why bring in the giant? This requires a second interpretation of
reading as speech. Reading is not merely other-directed. Reading is a
form of attention to phenomena that so involves investments in both the
text and the world that it also becomes a paradigm for certain attitudes
toward the self. Some texts lead us to desire not only a deeper grasp of
the world projected but a fuller identification with the power of what we
might call the textualized author. As the "I" awakens, it finds its own
investments so fully realized in a verbal structure that it desires the full
life that may be available there. Like Penelope with Ulysses (CP 520–21)
or the lover with his interior paramour (CP 524), we find ourselves projecting before us a deeper or richer way of sharing the intensity in the

gathering and unifying power of the author. Reading can be desiring to become, or glimpsing ourselves becoming, a certain kind of person figured as possible by the activity as well as by the content of a text. Read in a certain way, a world becomes alive – requiring in those who can find a language for it a certain kind of heroism, and, more important, making evident a virtual site where idealizing desires are inherently part of a commonal. As one reads, one sees what is available equivalently to all readers.

By such identifications, reading also fulfills one final function. It becomes the means by which we understand how we master repetition (CP 406), because it makes repetition the stage on which we come to recognize the forms of our basic desires, so that we can measure the intensifications accompanying a confidence that our reactions "fit" their context. Just as perception invites a sense of sections "collecting toward the greenest cone," reading produces a sense of ourselves fully inhabiting the forms of desire that most articulately give voice to the world. We become, in effect, "like rubies reddened by rubies reddening" (CP 346) because our "reddening" intensifies our capacity to participate in what cannot change, but what can appear as a new emblem for our own powers. Even if one does not forgive my stretching a pun, we still have in this statement a marvelous blend of intractable materiality permeated by an organic process of ripening. What endures can elicit increasingly fine, more resonant modes of response.

VIII

Reading is ultimately an Idealist ideal, with little to offer one concerned with social analysis or the articulation of specific political interests. Yet it has consequences somewhat different from those emphasized in typical Idealist aesthetics. The emphasis is not on heroic creative acts that appropriate the world under some single synthetic compositional force. There are dreams of appropriation, but they project a greenest cone formed out of powers we all share, powers we can even imagine forming a community around. Reading has a teleology that runs counter to individualist self-assertions. More important, reading is not a monistic principle. It idealizes shared powers, which themselves depend on worlds at once as intractable as minerals and as fertile as the *as* can make them. Thus Stevens can imagine a secular giant hovering over worlds far less overtly sublime than Chocorua's, as in "The House Was Quiet and the World Was Calm":

The house was quiet and the world was calm.
The reader became the book; and summer night

Was like the conscious being of the book.
The house was quiet and the world was calm. . . .

The quiet was part of the meaning, part of the mind:
The access of perfection to the page.

And the world was calm. The truth in a calm world,
In which there is no other meaning, itself

Is calm, itself is summer and night, itself
Is the reader leaning late and reading there.   (CP 358–59)

Here the abstract rendering of powers becomes a permission for total
investment in the world as it is. This permission will not satisfy all our
desires, but it makes an excellent beginning. Because it must be abstract,
the scene can place calmness under a stylistic aspect endowing it with
enormous energy. One becomes master of repetition here by letting it
constitute the focal point for the brilliant syntactic shifts of the closing
lines. Repetitions of single words (as opposed to the poem's earlier refrain
effects) produce a sharp break with the dominant pattern of end-stopped
lines. Syntax is suspended, only to speed up in very brief clauses. Then,
as time turns back against itself, as reading self-consciously repeats its
world and decides that it is good, it finds its culminating expression in a
series of present participles transforming all that calm into a pure state
for which the reading stands as its perfection. Confronting such a present, the sympathetic reader becomes absorbed in a corresponding activity. "There" and "here," the scene and the projected reader, then the
projected reader and the actual reader, become dialectical functions of
one another, all as exponents of this single figure who proleptically represents one hundred eyes seeing at once, and finding that we must lean
further into this enchanting site. Anywhere becomes everywhere, and
everywhere the basis of romance. Now one hundred and fifty years of
Romantic quest leads to the plainest of propoundings. When abstraction
can so intensify the powers involved, there need be no anxiety requiring
the deferral of hidden intentions or dramatic substitutes for one's plain
sense of things. Poetry can be transparent, paradoxically, because the
burden is not on its truth but on the intense force in the present which
the poem displays as it interprets, and hence takes responsibility for. And
once propoundings become transparent, we can "read words spoken as
if there was no book." The words themselves create an abstract space of

such elemental sounds that one feels reading given the same concrete presence in the work and in the world that color and line give to sight. Reading poetry there provides a substantial theory for living here. ·

NOTES

1   My comments on the new critical historicist attitudes to literature are directed more against a general stance than against specific Stevens critics. For this attitude applied to Modernism see Terry Eagleton, *Criticism and Ideology* (London: Vernon Editions, 1978), chapter 4, and Charles Harrison, "The Ratification of Abstract Art," in Michael Compton, ed., *Towards a New Art: Essays on the Background of Abstract Art* (London: Tate Gallery, 1980). The criticism of Stevens has not yet taken up the arguments the new historicism poses. Nor can it, I suspect, so long as it remains dominated by three attitudes, none of which is capable of describing the roles abstraction plays in his poetry or that his poetry might play in our lives. For example, Harold Bloom's Nietzschean Stevens in pursuit of an imperial self engages in dramas it is impossible to socialize at all. At the other extreme, the Stevens of Helen Vendler's *Part of Nature, Part of Us* (Cambridge, Mass: Harvard Univ. Press, 1980) is all too typical of contemporary society's willingness to identify with the august imagination only when it is "checked, baffled, frustrated, and reproved" (pp. 41–42). Finally, Joseph Riddel's Deconstructionist Stevens, who seeks "a writing that kills" by constantly disclosing the artifice in our fictions (p. 335), never ceases from decreation long enough to adopt a stance one can demystify or, one must add, that society can care about as a fiction. For Bloom and Riddel see, respectively, *Wallace Stevens: The Poems of Our Climate* (Ithaca: 1977) and "Metaphoric Staging: Stevens' Beginning Again of the 'End of the Book'," in Frank Doggett and Robert Buttel, eds., *Wallace Stevens: A Celebration* (Princeton: Princeton Univ. Press, 1980). The effects of these traditions are clearest in Marjorie Perloff's fascinating "Pound/Stevens: Whose Era?", *New Literary History* 13 (1982), 485–514, where, among many other claims, she uses Stevens' critics to suggest that there is nothing distinctively modern about his work (see, e.g., p. 504). Perloff may be right about his critics; however, I hope to show here that Stevens' many comments on his own modernity deserve to be taken quite seriously and quite literally.

2   Wallace Stevens, *The Necessary Angel: Essays on Reality and the Imagination* (London: Faber and Faber, 1951), p. 29. Hereinafter cited as NA.

3   I give a more elaborate account of this pressure in my description of a tension between lucidity and lyricism basic to post-Enlightenment culture. See my *Sense and Sensibility in Contemporary American Poetry* (New York: Cambridge Univ. Press, 1984), chapter 1.

4   Wallace Stevens, *The Collected Poems of Wallace Stevens* (New York: Knopf, 1954), p. 516. Hereinafter cited as CP.

5   I develop Stevens' "theory" of metaphor as one providing an alternative to

standard complex reference theories, and hence as a form of dealing with the embodiment of powers, in my "Wallace Stevens' Metaphors of Metaphor: Poetry as Theory," *American Poetry* 1 (1983), 27–48. This work on Stevens has as its context a series of my essays developing the concept of abstraction throughout Modernism: "Abstraction as Act: Modernist Poetry in Relation to Painting," *Dada/Surrealism* 10–11 (1982), 106–34, defines abstraction and shows how Williams, Apollinaire, Eliot, and Yeats all contribute ways of realizing Modernist forms of abstraction. "Representation, Representativeness and 'Non-Representational' Art," *Journal of Comparative Literature and Asthetics* 5 (1982), 1–23, shows how Malevich employs for semantic purposes what I here call presentational strategies. "Picasso's Collages and the Force of Cubism," *Kenyon Review* n.s. 6 (1984), 8–33, concentrates on how these strategies so organize mental energies that their working as portents of our powers becomes the thematic force of the work. These essays in turn take much of their context from the following materials: Leo Steinberg, *Other Criteria* (New York: Oxford Univ. Press, 1972); Marcelin Pleynet, *Système de la Peinture* (Paris: Editions du Seuil, 1977); Harold Osborne, *Abstraction and Artifice* (London: Oxford Univ. Press, 1979); Wendy Steiner, *Exact Resemblance to Exact Resemblance: The Literary Portraiture of Gertrude Stein* (New Haven: Yale Univ. Press, 1978) and *The Colors of Rhetoric* (Chicago: Univ. of Chicago Press, 1982). Steiner is especially good on the relation between depicting and displaying, but she shies away from fully thematic readings of what that relation makes available. Finally I want to mention a fine essay, B. J. Leggett, "Why It Must Be Abstract: Stevens, Coleridge, and I. A. Richards," *Studies in Romanticism* 22 (1983), 489–515, which I came upon too late to discuss in the essay.

6   Piet Mondrian, *Plastic and Pure Plastic Art* (New York: Wittenborn, 1945), pp. 116, 117, 119, 120, 121, 122.

7   Mondrian, "Natural Reality and Abstract Reality," in Herschel B. Chipp, ed., *Theories of Modern Art* (Berkeley: Univ. of California Press, 1976). The quotation from Pach is from *The Masters of Modern Art* (New York: W. B. Huebsch, 1924), p. 11. Pach's book, a copy of which (now at the Huntington Library) he gave to Stevens, makes evident the early Modernist sense of abstract art as an art of the mind's power – or, as the dust jacket statement by Elie Faure puts it, of how "the spiritual plane has progressively replaced the plane of nature." Stevens' own sense of how a theory of nonobjective painting might be formulated can be found in his remarks on Dufy and Gromaire (Wallace Stevens, *Opus Posthumous*, ed. Samuel French Morse [New York: Knopf, 1957], pp. 286–92; hereinafter cited as OP).

8   *The Letters of Wallace Stevens*, ed. Holly Stevens (New York: Knopf, 1966), p. 762.

9   Michel Benamou, "Wallace Stevens: Some Relations between Poetry and Painting," *Comparative Literature* 11 (1959), especially p. 49. Also very appropriate for Stevens' early materialism is a letter from Robert McAlmon, Sept. 2, 1921, at the Huntington Library.

10 "Modelled" could also refer to seeing pears as if they were in a painting; but

that reading simply does not allow the same richness, and it produces few significant differences from my own.

11 I find it theoretically interesting that it is the minimal reference of "blobs" that most emphatically creates the kind of space that perceptions cannot exhaust. Connotation does more than metaphor can to make perception lead to man.

12 It is typical of Stevens to emphasize self-referential uses of indices to define the authority upon which a poem's conclusion is based. See, for example, "An Ordinary Evening in New Haven" and "A Primitive Like an Orb."

13 Stevens' closest parallel to the method as well as the message in Wittgenstein's late reflections on the *as* is found in a prose passage on how the imagination transforms the site of a homecoming (NA 129–30). For one philosophical essay providing a rich poetic sense of the *as* in Wittgenstein, see Francis Sparshott, " 'As' or the Limits of Metaphor," *New Literary History* 6 (1974), 75–94.

14 I have used the following works of Wittgenstein: *Notebooks 1914–16*, trans. G. E. M. Anscombe (New York: Harper Torchbooks, 1969) abbreviated in text as N; *Philosophical Investigations*, trans. G. E. M. Anscombe (New York: Macmillan, 1958) abbreviated in text as PI; and *Tractatus Logicus Philosophicus*, trans. D. F. Pears and B. F. McGuiness (London: Routledge and Kegan Paul, 1961), abbreviated as TLP.

II

Stevens as Context

6

The "Community of Elements" in Wallace Stevens and Louis Zukofsky

ALAN GOLDING

On April 29, 1971, a speaker rose at the University of Connecticut to deliver the eighth annual Wallace Stevens Memorial Lecture. That speaker was not Helen Vendler or Joseph Riddel, both authors of what were even then canonical books on Stevens. It was not a Stevensian poet like Richard Wilbur or John Hollander. It was Louis Zukofsky – the same Zukofsky who is rarely discussed in the same room, let alone the same sentence, as Stevens. In none of the major criticism on Stevens – by Vendler, Riddel, J. Hillis Miller, A. Walton Litz, Harold Bloom – is Zukofsky even mentioned. By the same token, in the index to Barry Ahearn's recent book on Zukofsky, Stevens is mentioned twice, while Williams is mentioned nine times and Pound twelve. In Lazlo Géfin's history of the Imagist and Objectivist traditions, Stevens is not mentioned at all.[1] Williams and Pound are the poets with whom Zukofsky is usually linked, with Stevens considered the main representative of a contrary tradition. So Zukofsky appears a surprising choice to give the Stevens Memorial Lecture. But in fact he had an early interest in Stevens that has been obscured in critical discussions by his more intimate connections with the Pound–Williams Objectivist line. After his late rereading of Stevens, Zukofsky said, "[I] felt that my own writing . . . was closer to him than to that of any of my contemporaries in the last half century of life we shared together" (P 27).[2] And he acknowledged Stevens' *Harmonium* as one central influence during the 1920s and early 1930s, his formative years as a poet. The question I want to answer, then, is this: Given their apparently different thematic interests and stylistic affiliations, why should Zukofsky have felt so close to Stevens?

Certainly one must limit any claims for Stevens' influence on Zukofsky. Zukofsky never met Stevens, and they exchanged letters only once. This was over Zukofsky's use of Stevens' poem "Another Weeping

Woman" in the 1948 anthology *A Test of Poetry* (his version of *ABC of Reading*) – a book to which Stevens responded quite favorably.[3] When Zukofsky was invited to Connecticut to give the memorial lecture, Stevens was not a voluntary topic. Marcella Booth (then Spann) had invited Zukofsky to win him some attention; the Stevens lecture was a convenient way to do that. Even so, George Butterick writes that Zukofsky "welcomed the opportunity to speak on Stevens, that he took the talk very seriously, that when it was pointed out that most of the poets in previous years who had given the 'lecture' actually only read their own poems, or with maybe a few of Stevens' thrown in, that that was quite acceptable – he still preferred to work up a lecture, spent some time the spring of 1971 making notes, etc."[4] Zukofsky's seriousness casts in a different light what might appear at first to be rather contrived biographical and literary connections between himself and Stevens. When he and Stevens both lived in New York, Zukofsky says, they "may have walked . . . and walked the same streets, past each other unknown" (P 28). In 1927 he *almost* met Stevens when he was interviewed for a job with Stevens' firm, the Hartford Indemnity Accident Company: "Before leaving I asked the receptionist if Mr. Stevens was in and he went back to ask and Mr. Stevens was away" (P 31). Elsewhere in the lecture Zukofsky seems to make sly jokes in which he questions the very idea of influence – his deadpan comment, for example, on his and Stevens' "use of horses and donkeys thruout our poems" (P 34).

Yet for all his dry humor, such coincidences had real meaning for Zukofsky. In his *Autobiography* he uses coincidence to connect "bare facts . . . historic and contemporary particulars" (P 12), suggesting a subtle community between himself and other writers:

> But the bare facts are: I was born in Manhattan, January 23, 1904, the year Henry James returned to the American scene to look at the Lower East Side. The contingency appeals to me as a forecast of the first-generation American infusion into twentieth-century literature. At one time or another I have lived in all of the boroughs of New York City – for over thirty years in Brooklyn Heights not far from the house on Cranberry Street where Whitman's *Leaves of Grass* was first printed.[5]

The Stevens lecture is packed with such contingencies. Once we understand their appeal to Zukofsky, they begin to seem less contrived and become simply an accurate way of describing his relationship to Stevens – a "partial coincidence or community of elements between two figures" (P 34), but a community that is no less real for being partial. This community of elements, I suggest, extends to areas more significant than the mutual use of horse and donkey imagery. It suggests some surprising general affinities between two American poetic traditions that we usually separate – the "Imagist–Objectivist" and "Symbolist" traditions.

Marjorie Perloff lays out the terms of the debate between these two traditions in an invaluable article, "Pound/Stevens: Whose Era?" First, she shows how critics of modern poetry tend to fall into two opposing critical camps and observes how "few participants in the Modernist debate . . . [have] written sympathetically of both Stevens and Pound" (PS 501). She then reviews the differing critical terminology typically used to discuss the two poets. Poundians generally focus on technique, using terms like "precision," "particularity," "image," "technique," "structure," "concreteness" (PS 496) – terms that recur in commentary on Zukofsky. Stevens' critics tend to focus not on *how* he writes but on *what* he writes about, on subject matter rather than form: they talk of "being," "consciousness," "fiction," "reality," "self," "truth," "imagination" (PS 492). Harold Bloom's value judgments on Stevens, for instance, "refer always to what the poet is saying rather than to how he says it" (PS 489). Finally, Perloff contrasts the two traditions on epistemological grounds, setting the Poundian "respect for the given, for the form of the object" against the "symbolist transformation of objects" (PS 503).[6]

Charles Altieri, in another essay on the two traditions, draws a similar epistemological distinction:

> On the most general level, there are probably two basic modes of lyric relatedness – symbolist and objectivist styles. The former stress in various ways the mind's powers to interpret concrete events or to use the event to inquire into the nature or ground of interpretive energies, while objectivist strategies aim to "compose" a distinct perceptual field which brings "the rays from an object to a focus." Where objectivist poets seek an artifact presenting the modality of things seen or felt as immediate structure of relations, symbolist poets typically strive to see beyond the seeing by rendering in their work a process of mediating [sic] upon what the immediate relationships in perception reflect.[7]

The important contrasts here are between "interpreting" or "inquiring" and "composing," and between "medi[t]ating" and "presenting." Later in his essay Altieri phrases the issue as a contrast between the measuring mind of the Objectivist poet and the interpretive mind of the Symbolist poet. While he does not place Stevens explicitly in the "interpretive" Symbolist tradition, other critics do: Walton Litz, following the poet's own lead, characterizes Stevens as an "introspective voyager," while Bloom values Stevens' work because it is so "advanced as *interpretation*."[8]

This view of Stevens stresses, with good reason, the interiority of his poetry, its element of "mental moonlight" (CP 36). Much in Stevens' work supports such a view, from the singer of "The Idea of Order at Key West" (CP 128) ordering the world through art, to the statement that it is only "au pays de la métaphore qu'on est poète" (OP 179). Most readers agree that Stevens' poetry represents a lifelong meditation on the relation between imagination and reality, but his adherence to the "reality" side of that relation sometimes gets short shrift. We forget that all of those famous statements in which Stevens celebrates the imagination can be matched by statements in which he celebrates a literal, physical reality, the world before it is transformed by imagination: "The imagination loses vitality as it ceases to adhere to what is real" (NA 6); "Reality is the central reference for poetry" (NA 71); "The pears are not viols, / Nudes or bottles. / They resemble nothing else. / . . . / The pears are not seen / As the observer wills" (CP 196–97). Indeed, it is Stevens himself who often seems to go farthest toward resolving the supposed conflict between fidelity to the imaginative world and fidelity to the literal world, a conflict that later readers have used to distinguish the Symbolist and Objectivist traditions. In a statement that Zukofsky valued highly, "The Noble Rider and the Sound of Words," Stevens speaks not of a conflict between the two ways of seeing but of an equilibrium: "The relation between the imagination and reality is a question, more or less, of precise equilibrium. Thus it is not a question of the difference between grotesque extremes." (NA 9) This precise equilibrium constitutes poetry, "an interdependence of the imagination and reality as equals" (NA 27).

Some of Stevens' work, and Zukofsky's interest in it, cuts across the Symbolist–Objectivist distinction in other ways. The Objectivist tradition is generally considered the tradition of American speech, a tradition originating with Whitman and perpetuated vociferously by Williams; Stevens is associated more often with a European rhetoric that somehow managed to avoid getting its neck wrung. One of the original Objectivist group, Carl Rakosi, has said that much as he loved Stevens as a young poet, the beauties of Stevens' poetry are not those of "a man talking" (I 198). Similarly, Zukofsky disapproved of Stevens when he found him "clambering the stiles of English influence" and sounding like Milton (P 139). In some of Stevens' poetry, however – he specifies "The Jack-Rabbit" (CP 50) as one example – Zukofsky found "a grass roots or local, often barbaric voice" that led him to call Stevens an "eccentric native genius," again bringing Stevens closer to Zukofsky's own camp: "Reading him I am led to hope that my own poems, though different, sound that native and kind . . . indigenous like Winslow Homer's palm tree in a Florida wind" (P 33). Nor is this view of a "native" and "indigenous" Stevens as idiosyncratic as it might sound. Remember that Crispin trains himself to write in "indigenous dew" (CP 31). Both Roy Harvey Pearce and Harold Bloom have placed Stevens squarely in the continuity of American poetry, relating him to Emerson; Bloom considers him our most representative American poet, a major proponent of the Emersonian First Idea.[9]

In his 1930 essay, "American Poetry 1920–1930," Zukofsky praises the "resonant elegance of precision" of Stevens' diction and includes *Harmonium* in a slim bibliography of worthwhile books of the 1920s (P 138). Although he did not read all of Stevens until later in life, he repeats in the memorial lecture that he "was interested in [Stevens] very early" (P 24). He was fascinated first by the language of Stevens' early plays, probably by the limpid simplicity and concreteness of diction in lines like these from *Three Travellers Watch a Sunrise:*

> Dew is water to see,
> Not water to drink:
> We have forgotten water to drink.
> Yet I am content
> Just to see sunrise again.
> I have not seen it
> Since the day we left Pekin.
> It filled my doorway,
> Like whispering women.   (OP 128)

Zukofsky went on to read avidly the other Stevens work published in *Poetry* magazine and in Harriet Monroe's anthology, *The New Poetry*. A few years later, he says, he "read *[Harmonium]* constantly" (P 30). In other words, he knew early Stevens backwards.

What Zukofsky valued in Stevens was "the words" (P 29) – the style, not the ideas; the manner, not the matter. As we have seen from Perloff's discussion of the issue, critics often invoke this distinction to differentiate the Stevens and Pound–Williams lines in twentieth-century poetry. Hugh Kenner sets Williams' interest in technique against Stevens' interest in paraphrasable content; Donald Davie argues that Stevens' style and content can be separated in a way that Pound's cannot.[10] But the distinction is no invention of critics. Williams and Stevens adhered to it themselves, quite emphatically. Williams' position is well known: "It isn't what [the poet] *says* that counts as a work of art, it's what he makes . . . What does it matter what the line 'says'?"[11] This position baffled Stevens, and some of his responses to it have themselves become notorious:

> Williams is an old friend of mine. I have not read Paterson. I
> have the greatest respect for him, although there is the constant

difficulty that he is more interested in the way of saying things than in what he has to say. The fact remains that we are always fundamentally interested in what a writer has to say. When we are sure of that, we pay attention to the way in which he says it, not often before. (L 544)

Stevens was ready to match his old friend dogma for dogma. He felt quite comfortable separating modern poetry into two classes, "one that is modern in respect to what it says, the other that is modern in respect to form" (NA 168). To summarize the division he contrasts Valéry (one of his own masters) and Apollinaire (one of Zukofsky's), stating rather sternly that "each one of these classes is intransigent as to the other" (NA 169).

Stevens aligned himself with the poetry "that is modern in respect to what it says." Zukofsky, however, repeatedly shows his distaste for what many readers value in Stevens, his philosophizing.[12] Zukofsky's long prose treatise, *Bottom: On Shakespeare,* "takes exception to all philosophies from Shakespeare's point of view," the point of view that "favors the clear physical eye against the erring brain" (P 167). He may even have had Stevens in mind when he wrote in *Bottom* that "some poetry has been involved in philosophy to the hurt of its own eyes."[13] Zukofsky felt that the clear, physical eye, registering the clear, physical image, made for what he called, borrowing Marianne Moore's phrase, " 'a greater accessibility to experience' " in poetry. By contrast he found in Stevens' work after *Harmonium* "an attenuated 'accessibility to experience' " (P 138). In a 1968 interview he remarks, "I don't see why Wallace Stevens ruined a great deal of his work by speaking vaguely about the imagination and reality and so on. He can be a wonderful poet, but so much of it is a bore, bad philosophy." (I 228) Finally, in his memorial lecture Zukofsky specifies that about 1936, when *Ideas of Order* appeared, he grew impatient with Stevens' use of the words "reality" and "imagination"; he "deferred reading the greater part of his work after admiring the early poems of *Harmonium*" (P 27). In other words, he turned his back on Stevens' central theme – the "war between the mind / And sky, between thought and day and night" (CP 407).

So Stevens' ideas did not impress, or even interest, Zukofsky. But his diction and music did – a surprising discovery, since Pound and Williams are rightly held to be Zukofsky's main stylistic influences, and they hardly resemble Stevens. Zukofsky used Stevens' ear to excuse the "bad philosophy": "His music thruout has not been impaired by having philosophized." (P 30) He thought Stevens a strong poet despite, not because of, his philosophizing. Coming from a poet who held throughout his

career that "naturally in a poem image, cadence, and idea are inseparable" (P 143), this separation of "music" and "philosophy" appears self-
contradictory. But in reading others, poets tend to take what they want
and leave the rest. Zukofsky, because he was most interested in what the
poet makes, naturally took a lesson about making even from Stevens,
someone more interested in what the poet says. If we look beyond
Zukofsky's late public reevaluation of Stevens to his lifelong poetic practice, we find he valued that poetry of Stevens – parts of *Harmonium,*
essentially – in which music and meaning can least easily be separated.
Zukofsky found in one aspect of Stevens' work something to reaffirm
the definition of poetry as song that he had already picked up from Pound's
writings on and translations of Provençal poetry. In so doing he partially
bridged the gap between the Stevens and the Pound–Williams views of
poetry, using his reading of Stevens to implement Pound's advice that
the budding poet "fill his mind with the finest cadences he can discover,
preferably in a foreign language, so that the meaning of the words may
be less likely to divert his attention from the movement."[14]

This identification of sound and meaning is central to Zukofsky's poetics,
then; and he valued those parts of Stevens' work that reinforced the identification. In discussing "Academic Discourse at Havana," for instance,
he concentrates on lines in which sound most vividly communicates idea:
on the sardonic, spitting plosives of "a peanut parody / For peanut people," on the relaxed, wavelike rhythm and breathy vowels of the iambic
pentameter "How full of exhalations of the sea" (CP 143, 144). Lines like
these fulfill Stevens' dicta from "Adagia" that language is "the material
of poetry not its mere medium or instrument" and that "the word must
be the thing it represents" (OP 171, 168). While these propositions sound
surprising coming from a poet who saw himself as more "sayer" than
"maker," Zukofsky would certainly subscribe to them.

One way the poet transforms word into thing is by emphasizing the
word's aural texture. In *Harmonium* especially Stevens treated the word
physically sounded as an object to be held up for attention, rather in the
way that Charles Olson proposed later in his essay, "Projective Verse."
Stevens believed "that, above everything else, poetry is words; and that
words, above everything else, are, in poetry, sounds" (NA 32). Zukofsky viewed language the same way. "I like to keep the noises as close to
the body as possible," he says; "the word is so much of a physiological
thing that its articulation, as against that of other words, will make an
'object'." (I 218) In *Bottom,* that apparently philosophical treatise written
"to do away with all philosophy" (I 216) which he saw as "a continua-
tion of [his] work on prosody" (P 167), Zukofsky maintained "that even
the most intellective of [words] are tangible" (P 172). From this point of

view, much of the almost nonsensical diction and exaggerated alliteration of *Harmonium* must have made perfect sense to Zukofsky – concrete, physical sense. In a 1938 poem Zukofsky described his work as "songs / straining at sense" (All 89) – sense as meaning, but also sense as physical presence. Zukofsky shared Stevens' attention to syllables as physical, sensual, aural entities, often unburdened by "sense" in the sense of "meaning." As Williams says to a frustrated interviewer in *Paterson*, "Sometimes modern poets ignore sense completely."[15]

On this issue of sense, it is worth taking issue briefly with the view of Stevens that Hugh Kenner offers in *The Pound Era* and *A Homemade World*, because that view is an influential but I think misguided one. While Kenner sees Zukofsky's ear for odd diction as implying a care for language as physiological gesture – something I wouldn't disagree with – he calls the same feature of Stevens' work "the adolescent's delight in queer words."[16] Often Stevens has no more substance than Edward Lear or Lewis Carroll, Kenner says; he aspires merely to make a world of words. This dismissal stems from a failure to see the seriousness in Stevens' apparent nonsense. Zukofsky differs from Kenner on this point, and his own observation about Carroll, whom he admired, could easily apply to Stevens: "Carroll ultimately refused to commit himself as to whether his nonsense had any overt meaning. But the nonsense recorded its own testimony." (P 65) Zukofsky saw that Stevens' nonsense represents a celebration of the physical world, including the physical aspects of language. It embodies what Irvin Ehrenpreis calls, in a useful essay on this topic, "a feeling of intimacy with reality" – the kind of intimacy that would appeal to an Objectivist and that Zukofsky found lacking in much of Stevens' later work.[17]

Stevens' attention to the materiality of language as a way to gain an "intimacy with reality," his "verbal mimetic reproduction . . . of the actual density of the physical world," is central to the community of elements between him and Zukofsky.[18] James Rother observes how, in his use of nonsense syllables, Stevens attempts "to confer upon each image or sound the tactile presence of a substance in space, using techniques analogous to Zukofsky's 'objectivism'."[19] One such technique is "sincerity," which Zukofsky defined thus: "[The poet's] ear is sincere, if his words convey his awareness of the range of differences and subtleties of duration." (P 23) As a critical dictum this sounds rather limp: sincerity means having a good ear. But as an element of the community that Zukofsky felt between himself and Stevens, the idea of prosodic sincerity, of care for duration, is important. Duration is after all the very quality that Zukofsky uses Stevens to demonstrate in *A Test of Poetry*.

To suggest examples of Stevens' influence on Zukofsky's music, I will turn first to some poems from *All,* Zukofsky's collected short poems. In 1926 he wrote "Poem beginning 'The'," which contained this passage:

> Hard, hard, the cat-world.
> On the stream Vicissitude
> Our milk flows lewd.
>
> We'll cry, we'll cry,
> We'll cry the more
> And wet the floor,
>
> Megrow, megrow,
> Around around,
> The only sound
>
> The prowl, our prowl,
> Of gentlemen cats
> With paws like spats
>
> Who weep the nights
> Till the nights are gone –
> – And r-r-run – the Sun!   (All 17)

How close the obtrusively absurd rhymes, patterning, and repetition are to passages like this one from Stevens' "The Ordinary Women":

> The lacquered loges huddled there
> Mumbled zay-zay and a-zay, a-zay.
> The moonlight
> Fubbed the girandoles.
>
> And the cold dresses that they wore,
> In the vapid haze of the window-bays,
> Were tranquil
> As they leaned and looked
>
> From the window-sills at the alphabets,
> At beta b and gamma g,
> To study
> The canting culicues
>
> Of heaven and of the heavenly script
> And there they read of marriage bed.
> Ti-lill-o!
> And they read right long.   (CP 11)

Although Zukofsky never aspired to the scale of statement that this last stanza contains, the effect of both passages can be summed up in Zukofsky's lines, "for you I have emptied the meaning / Leaving the song" (All 89).

In a 1937 poem, "Motet," Zukofsky turned Stevensian nonsense rhymes to satirizing the military: "General Martinet Gem Coughed A-hem, and A-hem, and A-hem Deploying the nerves of his men Right, and about face, to his phlegm. Their whangs marched up to the sky, His eyes telescoped in his head A pollow that as pillar of Europe He flung to his rupture A-head" (All 212). Briefer examples of Stevensian sound play can be found in such poems as "No One Inn" (1932) – "the windings an inn / the windings a face in an inn / the windings no one is in in No One Inn" (All 64) – and in this from a 1941 poem: "And so till we have died / And grass with grass / Lie faceless as the grass" (All 96). In 1959 Zukofsky sums up what he has learned of poetic measure: *"Look in your own ear and read"* and "don't run to mind / boys' Greeks' metres gnomes." The allusion is to Pound, but the sound recalls Stevens: "rummage in tee tomes, tee-tums, tum-tees. / Forget terms" (All 216). The poem is informed not only by Pound's warning against metronomes but also by Stevens' "Ploughing on Sunday": "Tum-ti-tum, / Ti-tum-tum-tum! / The turkey-cock's tail / Spreads to the sun." (CP 20)

It is clear from these examples that the sounds of *Harmonium* rang in Zukofsky's ear throughout his career. When he lectured on Stevens, he implicitly reaffirmed the influence of Stevens' ear on his own work. That lecture concluded with Zukofsky's reading of six Stevens poems and six of his own. Of the Zukofsky poems, three promote pure sound over sense. One is the beginning of "A"-15, which when read aloud makes the reader pronounce the Hebrew sounds of the Book of Job. It contains passages like this:

Wind: Yahweh at Iyyob
Mien His roar 'Why yammer
Measly makes short hates oh
By milling bleat doubt?
Eye sore gnaw key heaver haul its core
Weigh as I lug where hide any?   (A 359)

Another selection takes off from the *Book of Taliesin:*

o Nine wreathe'll laugh & knot
o fruit of fruit thew
o fruit to deck or root
o really a blood hue brae
o flight gie to goad dew
o preed o preed rath

(The speaker of this passage is the character Dala in Zukofsky's novel, *Little*. When Dala is asked by his son Little what he is doing, he replies "Welshing" – making up a language that sounds like Old Celtic.) Zukofsky also read one of his phonetic translations from Catullus – in which, for instance, he renders Catullus' "quascumque" as "kiss come to" and "atque ero" as "I choir."[20] In each of these selections Zukofsky read an English phoneticization of a foreign or dead language. Clearly his interest in this poetry lay more in sound than in paraphrasable meaning, and this interest can be traced partly to his reading of Stevens. Although one root of this aspect of Zukofsky's style is Pound's Provençal translations, another is lines like Stevens' "bid him whip / In kitchen cups concupiscent curds" and "Chieftain Iffucan of Azcan in caftan / Of tan with henna hackles, halt!" (CP 64, 75) Again, Stevens confirmed a poetic procedure that Zukofsky had learned from Pound.

Before reading his own poems, however, Zukofsky read six of Stevens', from all phases of that poet's career. His selection silently reasserts both his early distaste for Stevens' philosophizing and his preference for the side of Stevens that one would expect an Objectivist poet to appreciate: the Stevens who celebrated the literal, the physical, the external. First Zukofsky read "From the Misery of Don Joost," in which the weary speaker says "my body, the old animal, / knows nothing more" than "the senses and feeling, the very sound / And sight, and all there was of the storm" (CP 46). He also chose "Extraordinary References," in which poetry is made up of "the extraordinary references / Of ordinary people, places, things" that "compose us in a kind of eulogy" (CP 369). In this poem the world makes the poet as much as the poet makes the world. As Stevens says in "Anecdote of Men by the Thousand," "the soul . . . is composed / Of the external world" (CP 51). The world makes the poet again in Zukofsky's next selection, "The Planet on the Table," in which Stevens says "his poems, although makings of his self, / Were no less makings of the sun. // Some lineament or character / . . . / Of the planet of which they were part." (CP 532–33) I suspect Zukofsky chose "Song of Fixed Accord" mainly for its vowel play and alliteration, for lines like "Rou-cou spoke the dove, / Like the sooth lord of sorrow, / Of sooth love and sorrow." But even in this poem, a rather sorry and muted dove accepts with cooing regret the "ordinary glare" of the literal, "like a fixed heaven, // Not subject to change" (CP 519–20).

If Zukofsky's choice of poems condemns by exclusion Stevens' epistemological meanderings, it also shows Stevens to have more affinities with the Imagist and Objectivist traditions than we usually admit. Stevens distrusted "the lunatic of one idea / In a world of ideas" (CP 325). He liked the play of possibilities. But one possibility, which recurred throughout his lifelong debate between the literal and the imaginative worlds, was an almost Imagistic commitment to capturing an external physical reality. If he never espoused that possibility fully because he felt it limited a poet's choice of subject (OP 220), he also never denied that it could yield poetry: "Imagism is an ancient phase of poetry. It is something permanent." (OP 253) Writing to Williams, he remarks, "Given a fixed point of view, realistic, imagistic, or what you will, everything adjusts itself to that point of view; and the process of adjustment is a world in flux, as it should be for a poet."[21]

Williams especially, and to a lesser extent Marianne Moore, affected one area of Stevens' work as powerfully as they affected Zukofsky's, and these common sources help explain further Zukofsky's appreciation of *Harmonium.* Williams, Moore, and Stevens all reviewed each other's work favorably; and despite their celebrated spat over the poetic and the anti-poetic, Williams and Stevens maintained a lifelong friendship and correspondence. So, too, did Stevens and Moore; and it was Moore who reported to Celia Zukofsky in 1962 that Stevens had read and liked Louis' work.[22] In the work of Williams and Moore, which is often described as "realistic, imagistic, or what you will," Stevens found the synthesis of imaginary gardens and real toads that he pursued in his own work.[23] That is to say, he found value in just that poetic tradition, the Imagist–Objectivist tradition, that much subsequent criticism has set him against.

In fact Stevens' unpublished early work suggests that he independently developed certain Imagist principles of composition as early as 1909. These principles were reinforced by his close association with Williams during the peak years of Imagism, around 1913–17, when Stevens was writing much of *Harmonium.* That devout Imagist Amy Lowell admired "The Silver Plough-Boy" and "Peter Quince at the Clavier" when they appeared in *Others;* and she even gave "From the Journal of Crispin," an early draft of "The Comedian as the Letter C," first honorable mention in a poetry contest.[24] In 1935 Stevens wrote that "when *Harmonium* was in the making there was a time when I liked the idea of images and images alone, or images and the music of poetry together" (L 288). Indeed, one of the first writers on Stevens described him as a "musical imagist."[25] So the appeal that *Harmonium* eventually held for the Objectivist Zukofsky is not surprising. Many of its poems – "Earthy Anecdote," "The Load of Sugar Cane," "Tea," "Thirteen Ways of Looking at a Black-bird" (CP 3, 12, 112, 92) – read like Williams' snippets of Americana, or like the Poundian Imagist exercises from which Zukofsky learned so much. And in commenting on this work, Stevens goes to some lengths to stress his desire for concrete effects. In "Earthy Anecdote," he says, "I intended something quite concrete: actual animals"; and he adds that there is "no symbolism" in the poem. (L 209, 204)

For another source that Zukofsky and Stevens share, one relevant particularly to their use of strange or playful language, we can turn from imagism to Whitman. For Zukofsky, Whitman is a fairly clear ancestor: in the writing of the all-inclusive, lifelong poem that embraced his culture; in his exhaustive attention to the "historic and contemporary particulars" of that culture; in his ambition to embody in poetry, in Zukofsky's own words, "that order that of itself can speak to all men" (P 8). Predictably, Zukofsky valued Whitman's immersion in physical reality, "the raw Whitman who . . . 'descended upon things to arrest them all' and 'arrested' them 'all faithful solids and fluids' "(P 142). And in appending Whitman's "Respondez!" to the original edition of "A"-12, Zukofsky seems to have seen himself as one of Whitman's "Poets to Come." In 1927 he responded by taking up the cause of the poor, employing a Whitmanian long line:

> I look around at the economic appointors of my generation.
> These pretend not to notice me,
> Models of politeness and subterfuge they are;
> And feeling myself of the natural forces to come, for
>   appointors, I suppose I have what displaces them.
> Or at least being of the same quality as running water, for
>   appointors, I have no pity.[26]

And a few years later, in "A"-2, he invoked Whitman's metaphor for the writing of a long poem: "Faces and forms, I would write / you down / In a style of leaves growing." (A 8)

Few poets, by contrast, appear less alike than Whitman and Stevens. But once we look beyond Stevens' more obvious French influences, Whitman is a central source for his poetry. This case has been made by Pearce, Bloom, Joseph Riddel, Samuel French Morse, and in a whole book by Diane Wood Middlebrook.[27] Even if Stevens' reading of Whitman is one of Bloomian "misprision," beneath the clear differences do lie real similarities: the vision of the life's work as a single long poem; the aspiration to voice into being the democratic, humanist ideal, the "impossible possible philosophers' man"; the assumed power of poetry to bring out the ideal in the real. When reading, in fact, Stevens was not averse to making of his own poetry sound like Whitman's, as Robert Creeley reported to Charles Olson: "One time heard Stevens read, simply list of 'objects'."[28]

Whitman's presence in Stevens' work is most powerfully apparent in

"The Comedian as the Letter C." If the history of twentieth-century American poetry is indeed a series of arguments with Whitman, as Pearce has argued, then "Comedian" represents Stevens' argument with Whitman at its most intense, an argument between the two sides of Crispin/Stevens, the aesthete and "him that postulated as his theme / The vulgar" (CP 35). In this dialogue with himself, Stevens considers the possibility that underlies the whole Objectivist poetic – that the real, seen without the shadows cast by the imagination's "mental moonlight," could yield what Whitman's work often contains, a refreshed vision of the apparently mundane, "prose / More exquisite than any tumbling verse" (CP 37). Stevens may never be a realist *in propria persona,* as Williams once said, but in the person of Crispin he proposes a Whitmanian aesthetic, as well as in the "deluging onwardness" (CP 45) of the appositional syntax that he took from Whitman and made his own. Lines like the following make it hard to accept Williams' statement, in his obituary notice on Stevens, that Stevens had no interest in Whitman:[29]

> an aesthetic tough, diverse, untamed,
> Incredible to prudes, the mint of dirt,
> Green barbarism turning paradigm.   (CP 31)

Like *Leaves of Grass,* this aesthetic grows out of American soil (it is "the mint of dirt") and offers as a paradigm for poetry a "green barbarism" that recalls Whitman's "barbaric yawp."

Beyond these general affinities between Whitman and Zukofsky and between Whitman and Stevens to Zukofsky runs a tendency toward what one might call stylistic Adamism – the desire of many American poets to reinvent the language in every generation, to treat it as a new world, as a realm of exotic surprises open for exploration and discovery.[30] When Crispin arrives in America, he finds "a still new continent in which to dwell" and "make a new intelligence prevail" (CP 37). Part of the Supreme Fiction is the possibility of returning to "an immaculate beginning . . . that ever-early candor" (CP 382). This attitude often leads in poetry to a pleasure in alien-sounding diction. In Whitman and Stevens this can take the form of arrays of improbable names and nicknames – names like Monongahela, Kanuck, Tuckahoe in Whitman; like Tallapoosa and Pascagoula in Stevens. And the game does not stop with the unearthing of these indigenous words. As Whitman says in *An American Primer,* "these States are rapidly supplying themselves with new words," and he uses this fact as a license to invent foreign-sounding neologisms like "eclaircise" and "dolce affetuoso."[31] The same cast of mind reveals itself in such Stevens phrasings as "fubbed the girandoles," that sound composed of neologisms even when they are not, and in his habit of combining extremes of diction, the emphatically foreign and the emphatically native: "exit lex, / Rex, and principium, exit the whole / Shebang" (CP 36–37). Zukofsky's approach to language is similarly Adamic, open to discovery. Like Whitman and Stevens, he makes up his own dialects ("Welshing") and delights in the "aleatorical indeterminate" (All 225). "I'm interested in the sound of words." (I 229) He is interested in words especially at their birth, when they first become physical formations of sounds and shapes and before they acquire meaning and associations. In "A"-12 Zukofsky describes the birth of language in terms drawn from Genesis:

> So goes: first, *shape*
> The creation –
> A mist from the earth,
> The whole face of the ground;
> Then *rhythm* –
> And breathed breath of life;
> Then *style* –
> That from the eye its function takes –   (A 126)

A number of Zukofsky's other poems self-referentially concern their own birth, their own coming into being as structures of sound: "The lines of this new song are nothing / But a tune making the nothing full." (All 97)

    Charles Bernstein criticizes Objectivism generally as an Adamic poetic, "filled with nostalgia for a primal world of instant, unmediated perception, severing eyes from the mind and from memory."[32] This argument contains some truth, but only some. For what Bernstein considers an Objectivist's naïve commitment to *res* in Zukofsky is complicated by a Stevensian or "Symbolist" playfulness with *verba,* and by Zukofsky's treatment of *verba* as physical objects, as themselves *res.* If Zukofsky favors a "*style* – / That from the eye its function takes,*"* and if that eye sometimes seems severed from mind, nevertheless the eye is joined with the ear in sophisticated ways:

>   I's (pronounced eyes)
> Hi, Kuh
>
> those
> gold'n bees
> are I's
>
> eyes,
>
> skyscrapers.   (All 71)

In this poem the "I" is led by the ear to become an "eye" (recalling Stevens' "the poet . . . is composed / Of the external world"), and the "eye" is led to the perception of the skyscrapers both by aural ("eye"– "sky") and by visual rhyme (the skyscraper as a giant "I" shape). Zukofsky has it both ways here. He emphasizes the aural texture of his language, turning *verba* into *res;* but he goes beyond merely playing among signifiers, for in the background there remains something signified. "Hi, Kuh" is not just a self-consciously bad pun on "haiku": "You remember Elsie, Borden's cow? That's what I meant, and I greeted her up on the sign there: 'Hi, Kuh'." (I 229)

One of Zukofsky's most ardent admirers, Robert Creeley, once praised Stevens for "always going by the ear."[33] And that is how Zukofsky's poetry "goes." Like Whitman with Monongahela, like Stevens with Pascagoula, so Zukofsky with words like "clavicembalo": He is interested in the sound of the word. (Remember that to the boy Zukofsky, raised speaking Yiddish, English must have sounded as exotic as "fubbed the girandoles" does to a new reader of Stevens.) More than any other twentieth-century poet, Zukofsky aspired to return poetry to the condition of music; and music has no "meaning." Hence "A"-7:

> Bum pump a-dumb, the pump is neither bum
> Nor dumb, dumb pump uh! hum, bum pump o! shucks!
> (Whose clavicembalo? bum? bum? te-hum . . .
> Not in the say but in the sound's – hey-hey –
> The way to-day, Die, die, die, die, tap, slow,
> Die, wake up, up! up! O *Saviour,* to-day!
> Choose Jews' shoes or whose: anyway Choose! Go!   (A 41)

Beside this we might put Stevens' "Tum-ti-tum, / Ti-tum-tum-tum!" or "tink and tank and tunk-a-tunk-tunk" (CP 59). Such openness to linguistic play once led Robert Duncan to place Zukofsky and Stevens side by side as models for "the addition of the un / plannd for interruption" in poetry.[34]

What compelled Zukofsky, then, were specific features of Stevens' early style, not his thematic concerns or sensibility (both of which could be said, by contrast, to have influenced James Merrill or the 1984 Stevens Memorial Lecturer, John Ashbery). That style changed, of course; but each stage in Stevens' stylistic evolution nevertheless has its own manner, its own limited, definable set of recurring tropes. Because of this Stevens' styles are easily imitated, and they have been assumed not only by Zukofsky but by other poets in the Objectivist line with whom Stevens would seem to share little: Rakosi, Creeley, Charles Tomlinson, Clayton

Eshleman.[35] Stevens has served these poets as a kind of stylistic antiself, giving them access to a manner that their tradition finally leads them to reject. Generally, Objectivist poets have loved Stevens and left him. But the fact that one *can* demonstrate Stevens' importance to poets like Zukofsky and these others should lead us to rethink the relationship between the two traditions that we have learned to call, rather too patly, the Symbolist and the Objectivist. Where the two traditions often overlap, as we have seen, is in the area of melopoeia – the area where, as Stevens and Zukofsky often do, the poet can empty the meaning, leaving the song.

NOTES

1   Barry Ahearn, *Zukofsky's A: An Introduction* (Berkeley: Univ. of California Press, 1983); Laszlo K. Géfin, *Ideogram: History of a Poetic Method* (Austin: Univ. of Texas Press, 1982).

2   I use the following parenthetical abbreviations in the text: A–Louis Zukofsky, *A* (Berkeley: Univ. of California Press, 1978); All–Louis Zukofsky, *All: The Collected Short Poems, 1923–1964* (New York: Norton, 1971); CP–Wallace Stevens, *The Collected Poems of Wallace Stevens* (New York: Knopf, 1954); I–L.S. Dembo and Cyrena N. Pondrom, eds., *The Contemporary Writer: Interviews with Sixteen Novelists and Poets* (Madison: Univ. of Wisconsin Press, 1972); L–Wallace Stevens, *Letters of Wallace Stevens,* ed. Holly Stevens (New York: Knopf, 1966); NA–Wallace Stevens, *The Necessary Angel: Essays on Reality and the Imagination* (New York: Knopf, 1951); OP–Wallace Stevens, *Opus Posthumous* (New York: Knopf, 1957); P–Louis Zukofsky, *Prepositions: The Collected Critical Essays of Louis Zukofsky* (Berkeley: Univ. of California Press, 1981); PS–Marjorie Perloff, "Pound/Stevens: Whose Era?" *New Literary History* 13 (1982), 485–514.

3   On October 13, 1948, Stevens wrote to Zukofsky that *A Test of Poetry* does "pick up a particular interest," and that he had been thinking recently about "the absence of the element of interest in so much poetry." This letter is quoted by permission of the Harry Ransom Humanities Research Center, The University of Texas at Austin. Zukofsky quotes it in his lecture, remarking that he "was especially comforted by the word *particular* because it could have been *general*" (P 32).

4   Unpublished letter to the author, March 2, 1984, quoted with Mr. Butterick's permission.

5   Louis Zukofsky, *Autobiography* (New York: Grossman, 1970), p. 13.

6   For development of the issues discussed in this paragraph, see Marjorie Perloff, *The Poetics of Indeterminacy: Rimbaud to Cage* (Evanston, Ill.: Northwestern Univ. Press, 1983), where she places Stevens in a Symbolist tradition inherited from Baudelaire and Mallarmé, and Zukofsky in a contrary tradition represented by Pound and Williams.

7   Charles Altieri, "The Objectivist Tradition," *Chicago Review* 30 (Winter 1979), 68. In a related essay Altieri casts the debate in terms of the distinction between metonymic and metaphoric uses of language. See Charles Altieri, "Objective Image and Act of Mind in Modern Poetry," *PMLA* 91 (1976), 101–14.

8   A. Walton Litz, *Introspective Voyager: The Poetic Development of Wallace Stevens* (New York: Oxford Univ. Press, 1972); Harold Bloom, *Wallace Stevens: The Poems of Our Climate* (Ithaca: Cornell Univ. Press, 1977), p. 168.

9   Roy Harvey Pearce, *The Continuity of American Poetry* (Princeton: Princeton Univ. Press, 1961), especially pp. 376–419; Bloom, *Wallace Stevens,* passim.

10 Hugh Kenner, *A Homemade World: The American Modernist Writers* (New York: Knopf, 1975), pp. 50–90; Donald Davie, *The Poet in the Imaginary Museum: Essays of Two Decades,* ed. Barry Alpert (New York: Persea, 1977), pp. 11–17.

11 William Carlos Williams, *Selected Essays of William Carlos Williams* (New York: New Directions, 1969), p. 257.

12 His philosophizing, of course, is precisely what many readers of Stevens value. See, for example, Roy Harvey Pearce and J. Hillis Miller, eds., *The Act of the Mind: Essays on the Poetry of Wallace Stevens* (Baltimore: The Johns Hopkins Press, 1965). The editors' stated intention is "to take seriously Wallace Stevens' claims as a philosophical poet, and to study the implications, the range, and the import of those claims" (p. ix).

13 Louis Zukofsky, *Bottom: On Shakespeare* (Austin: Humanities Research Center, Univ. of Texas, 1963), vol. 1, p. 114.

14 Ezra Pound, *The Literary Essays of Ezra Pound,* ed. T. S. Eliot (New York: New Directions, 1968), p. 5. Zukofsky's 1929 essay," "Ezra Pound" (P 67–83), shows ample acquaintance with Pound's translations of and prose writings about Provençal poetry.

15 William Carlos Williams, *Paterson* (New York: New Directions, 1963), p. 225.

16 Kenner, *A Homemade World,* p. 51.

17 Irvin Ehrenpreis, "Strange Relation: Stevens' Nonsense," in Frank Doggett and Robert Buttel, eds., *Wallace Stevens: A Celebration* (Princeton: Princeton Univ. Press, 1980), p. 223. To add one noteworthy piece of trivia: the recent *Heath Guide to Literature,* ed. David Bergman and Daniel Mark Epstein (Lexington, Mass.: D. C. Heath, 1984), pp. 740–45, contains a section called "Poems of Nonsense and Music." The four poems in that section include one by Carroll ("Jabberwocky"), one by Stevens ("Bantams in Pine-Woods"), and one by Zukofsky (his translation of Catullus' "Poem No. 41").

18 Helen Vendler, *On Extended Wings: Wallace Stevens' Longer Poems* (Cambridge, Mass.: Harvard Univ. Press, 1969), p. 52.

19 James Rother, "American Nonsense and the Style of Wallace Stevens," *Bucknell Review* 23 (1977), 175.

20 The *Taliesin* adaptation comes from Louis Zukofsky, *Little: For Careenagers* (New York: Grossman, 1970), p. 119. For the original Taliesin text, see William F. Skene, [ed.], *The Four Ancient Books of Wales* (Edinburgh: Edmonston and Douglas, 1868), vol. 2, pp. 141–42. The Catullus is from

Celia and Louis Zukofsky, trans., *Catullus* (*Gai Valeri Catulli Veronensis liber*) (London: Cape Goliard, 1969), n.p.

21 Quoted in Williams, *Selected Essays*, p. 12.

22 Celia Zukofsky," "A Commemorative Evening for Louis Zukofsky," *American Poetry Review* 9 (January/February 1980), 26.

23 See Bernard Heringman, "Wallace Stevens: The Use of Poetry," in Pearce and Miller, eds., *The Act of the Mind*, p. 4.

24 Samuel French Morse, *Wallace Stevens: Poetry as Life* (New York: Pegasus, 1970), pp. 73, 98.

25 The best discussion of Stevens' involvement with Imagism is in Robert Buttel, *Wallace Stevens: The Making of* Harmonium (Princeton: Princeton Univ. Press, 1967). Paul Rosenfeld calls Stevens a "musical imagist" in *Men Seen: Twenty-Four Modern Authors* (New York: The Dial Press, 1925), p. 152.

26 Louis Zukofsky, "Preface – 1927," *The Exile* (Autumn 1928), 78.

27 Pearce, *Continuity of American Poetry*; Bloom, *Wallace Stevens*; Joseph Riddel, "Walt Whitman and Wallace Stevens: Functions of a 'Literatus'," *South Atlantic Quarterly* 61 (1962), 506–20; Morse, *Wallace Stevens*; Diane Wood Middlebrook, *Walt Whitman and Wallace Stevens* (Ithaca: Cornell Univ. Press, 1974). Bloom, for instance, argues that Whitman is "a pervasive . . . influence upon all of Stevens' major poetry" (p. 10) and that "Notes toward a Supreme Fiction" is the twentieth century's "Song of Myself" (p. 171).

28 Robert Creeley, *Charles Olson and Robert Creeley: The Complete Correspondence*, ed. George F. Butterick (Santa Barbara, Calif.: Black Sparrow, 1980–83), vol. 3, p. 21. Cf. Stevens' own comment on one aspect of Whitman's poetry, that "the poems in which he collects large numbers of concrete things . . . have a validity which, for many people, must be enough" (L 870–71).

29 Williams makes these comments in his obituary notice on Stevens, "Wallace Stevens," *Poetry* 87 (1956), 236, 238.

30 In developing my argument in this paragraph, I owe much to Kenner's discussion of the topic in *A Homemade World*, pp. 216–17.

31 Walt Whitman, *An American Primer with Facsimiles of the Original Manuscript*, ed. Horace Traubel (San Francisco: City Lights, 1970), p. 5.

32 Charles Bernstein, "Words and Pictures," *Sagetrieb* 2 (Spring 1983), 27. For the opposite position – that Zukofsky's poetics is a poetics not of presence but of absence – see Burton Hatlen, "Zukofsky, Wittgenstein, and the Poetics of Absence," *Sagetrieb* 1 (Spring 1982), 63–93. For a useful synthesis, one that accommodates both "mimetic" and "structuralist" readings of Poundian and Objectivist poetry, see Donald Davie, *"Res* and *Verba* in *Rock-Drill* and After," *Paideuma* 11 (1982), 382–94.

33 Creeley, *Correspondence*, vol. 2, p. 14.

34 Robert Duncan, "Letters for Denise Levertov: An A Muse Ment," *Black Mountain Review* 1 (Fall 1954), 21.

35 To specify some poems by the poets named that follow Stevens in various ways: Carl Rakosi, "Homage to Wallace Stevens," in *Amulet* (New York: New Directions, 1967), p. 74; Robert Creeley, "Poem for D. H. Lawrence" and "Divisions," in *The Collected Poems of Robert Creeley, 1945–1975* (Berke-

ley: Univ. of California Press, 1983), pp. 7, 33; Charles Tomlinson, "Nine Variations in a Chinese Winter Setting" and "Suggestions for the Improvement of a Sunset," in *Selected Poems 1951–1974* (New York: Oxford Univ. Press, 1978), pp. 2–4; Clayton Eshleman, "A Late Evening in July," in *What She Means* (Santa Barbara, Calif.: Black Sparrow, 1978), p. 179, and "Winding Windows" and "Cimmeria" in *Hades in Manganese* (Santa Barbara, Calif.: Black Sparrow, 1981), pp. 69, 112.

7

Notes beyond the *Notes:*
Wallace Stevens and
Contemporary Poetics

MICHAEL DAVIDSON

For Roy Harvey Pearce

In one of his first letters to Charles Olson, Robert Creeley quotes
with approval a definition of poetry given by Wallace Stevens: "Poetic
form in its proper sense is a question of what appears within the poem
itself . . . By appearance within the poem itself one means the things
created and existing there. . . ."[1] Creeley adds: "Basic. Yet they won't
see it, that it cannot be a box or a bag or what you will." Stevens' definition stayed with Creeley, and appeared in a later letter as part of a
harangue against the technical skills of W. H. Auden: "Anyhow, form
has now become so useless a term that I blush to use it. I wd imply a
little of Stevens' use (the things created *in* a poem and existing there . . .)
& too, go over into: the possible casts or methods for a way into a 'subject'."[2] Creeley then adds his own version of Stevens' definition in terms
that have become somewhat more familiar: "To make it clear: that form
is never more than an *extension* of content." The rest is literary history.
Creeley's remarks found their way into Olson's "Projective Verse" essay,
in which Olson proposes a physiological, oral poetry that would have
made Wallace Stevens wince. And although we tend to read that essay
in terms of Pound and Williams, it is interesting to note the important
role that Stevens played in the formation of what has become one of the
canonical texts of Postmodernist poetics.

Creeley's remarks, of course, are hardly original; they are basic to any
organicist theory and can be found in variant forms throughout Romantic
literature. What Stevens offered Creeley and his generation of poets was
a particular version of romantic organicism in which poetry evolves
according to laws discovered in the act of composition. The validity of
these laws does not end with the poem in some kind of Kantian disinter-

estedness. These laws replicate mental orders that cannot, because of the constraints of ordinary discourse, be articulated. The poet uses the poem to discover aspects of psychological and natural life that, while near to hand, are nevertheless mediated by alien rhetorics. Coleridge's definition of poetry as that which contains "in itself the reason why it is so, and not otherwise"[3] had been hardened into New Critical versions of autotelic form. Stevens reintroduced into theories of Romanticism what Coleridge elsewhere calls "form as proceeding,"[4] that might serve as a paradigm for more recent open-ended and processual modes. And although Stevens was not, himself, a prosodic innovator, he awakened poets to the sheer combustive potential of language pushed to its maximum semantic and acoustic potential. More important, Stevens explored as thoroughly as any poet of his generation the vital contingencies between poetic language and what he called "the exquisite environment of fact."[5] If Coleridge, Emerson, Dickinson, and Whitman are Stevens' most obvious forebears in this poetics, he is the poet who most significantly translates this heritage into the present day.

Wallace Stevens' influence on contemporary poets is so pervasive, in fact, that discussion is almost superfluous beyond the most generalized level. In a recent issue of *The Wallace Stevens Journal,* a number of poets were asked to comment on Stevens' impact on their writing, and the opinions expressed are as varied as the poets themselves.[6] Robert Creeley admires the "teasing clarity of his propositions, . . . the fact that words [become] such substance of a world 'out of whole cloth,' so to speak." David Ignatow respects Stevens' Whitmanian defiance of "this greyness that his eyes met everywhere." W. S. Merwin is intrigued by Stevens' landscapes, "at once familiar, a revelation, and a composition of unimaginable depths and richnesses." Richard Wilbur rejoices "in the versatile energy with which he faced the aesthetic challenge of every mood, place, and weather." Richard Hugo is even inspired by the photos of Stevens that appear on the dust jackets of his books. How is the genealogist of influence to reconcile the variety of such tributes into a common set of concerns?

We should know better, however, than to trust the overt testimony found in *festschriften.* The theory of influence is tainted, we have come to understand, by false notions of continuity and causality. We must look at the poems themselves – in the interstices of their rhetoric – for evidence not only of what they say *about* Stevens but what they forget to say, what they cannot, in order to be the poems they are, admit to themselves. The most famous version of this theory claims that "strong poets" willfully misread their predecessors in a kind of Oedipal rejection of authority and power. In order for the new poet to write, he must systematically destroy his precursors and create a place for himself. (I use the masculine pronoun to indicate that this battle seems so far to have been fought only among males.) The value of this act lies not in the poems thus created but in the dialogue established between and among poems. Influence, as Harold Bloom conceives it, "means that there are *no* tests, but only relationships *between* tests."[7] What is generated out of this anti-genealogical genealogy is less literary history than a kind of gnostic eschatology by which the death of poetry is forestalled and the life of sublimation maintained for another generation. The bounty of misprision, according to Bloom, is anxiety; and among strong poets there is much anxiety, particularly among belated modern American poets who must compensate all the more forcefully for their felt distance from an established tradition.[8]

Bloom's theory is particularly important for our subject since it offers a salutary critique of formalist as well as literary historical definitions of tradition, and because it emphasizes Stevens' central influence upon more recent poets like John Ashbery and A. R. Ammons. But according to Bloom, such "ephebes" are produced, as it were, by artificial insemination, so that even the most Stevensian of contemporary poets must deny his literary parent:

> I don't consider myself any avatar of Wallace Stevens. It's true that some of my earlier work sounds very much like Wallace Stevens, but I certainly don't think it does throughout, certainly not to the extent [Bloom] says it does, and I don't think Stevens would have thought so either.[9]

Ashbery would seem to be executing his own poetic clinamen in relation to Bloom, overcompensating for a reading that has locked him into one tradition at the expense of others. The poet who wrote the very Stevensian "Clypsydra" or "Fragment," so the reading has it, could not be the same who wrote "Europe" or the poems in *The Tennis Court Oath* (a fearful disaster, says Bloom). And the poet who in *Three Poems* and "Self-Portrait in a Convex Mirror" seems a logical heir to "An Ordinary Evening in New Haven" or "The Auroras of Autumn" could not, at the same time, be the heir to *Impressions d'Afrique, The Large Glass,* or *Tender Buttons.* Little wonder, then, that Ashbery should swerve so violently.

For all Bloom's virtues in reminding us of the problematic nature of influence as conceived along traditional historicist lines, he has severely limited the contextual field in which we may read literary history. A poet's development, according to his theory, may occur solely along psychopathological lines; there is no room for a history other than literary history and no room for value outside aesthetics. Whatever temporality may have been opened in the poem or evoked beyond the page is spatialized by "revisionary ratios" or tropes by which the poet swerves, empties out, purges, and reappropriates the tradition.[10] These ratios are rhetorical stations of the cross in a psychological quest romance that the poet cannot recognize for himself. Thus, only the critic may complete the hermeneutic circle begun by the poet, closing off the poem and the history in which it is produced. Finally, the very democratic ethos that lies within Bloom's exemplars (Whitman, Emerson, Stevens, Crane) is violated by the notion of the "strong poet," one who turns self-reliance into willful misappropriation.

It is important to our current understanding of Stevens that this Oedipalized version of influence be qualified, because it fails to address some of the important ways in which the poet has been read in the postwar period.[11] It limits the kind and scope of influence to those poets who most resemble him at the level of rhetorical surface. Ashbery obviously "looks like" Stevens; but one could also say that the nature of the younger poet's verbal play – the indeterminacy of his pronouns in *Three Poems,* for example – serves a very different purpose than that of the older poet. Stevens seldom reflects the kind of personal insecurity and crisis that one finds in Ashbery, even though both share a tendency toward a discursive, wandering style. At the same time, a poet like Louis Zukofsky, usually thought to extend directly from the Poundian tradition, is most like Stevens in his concern for the moral worth of poetic language, "an instant certainty of the words of a poem bringing at least two persons and then maybe many persons, even peoples together."[12] This is much like the Stevens who feels that the poet's role is "to help people to live their lives" (NA 29).

Having argued the inadequacies of Bloom's theory of influence, I would like to suggest an alternative reading of Stevens in the light of certain contemporary poets, using "Notes toward a Supreme Fiction" as a touchstone. Necessarily, my coverage of this large topic must remain somewhat schematic and my selection of poets limited. I am not proposing a theory of influence, but rather a study of elements in Stevens' poetics that have helped generate at least one tradition in postwar poetry. I would see his influence, in this regard, as occupying three general areas: the use of the long poem in producing a destructive or decreative poetics; the operational or performative use of language to create a philosophical poetry; and the transformation, by these means, of a poetry of "place" into a poetry of "occasions."

"Notes toward a Supreme Fiction" is a particularly appropriate poem with which to examine Stevens' influence since one of its primary concerns is pedagogy:

> Begin, ephebe, by perceiving the idea
> Of this invention, this invented world,
> The inconceivable idea of the sun.   (CP 380)

Yet Stevens' is a pedagogy without texts or instructions, without cultural markers or "luminous moments" – without, we might say, method. The young poet must "become an ignorant man again / And see the sun again with an ignorant eye." In a paradox that haunts all of American literature, from Emerson to the present, the new poet must read so that he shall no longer have to read again. His poetic act shall not be the artisanal fabrication of a self-sufficient world; rather, his task is a violent one, to "press / A bitter utterance from [his] writhing, dumb, // Yet voluble dumb violence" (CP 384). We recognize this poetic violence as that described in "The Noble Rider and the Sound of Words," "a violence from within that protects us from a violence without" (NA 36).

   If poetry is a destructive as well as instructive force, it is all the more so in Stevens' later work, where the pursuit of a supreme fiction is merged with an increasingly interrogative and discursive style. Whereas in the lyrics and exercises of *Harmonium* the poet wrote brilliant, often witty variations on philosophical matters, from the mid-1930s on his method was to dramatize the mind in its speculative acts. As Roy Harvey Pearce points out, the change in Stevens' later style is not a radical departure but represents a logical evolution from the problems advanced in his early lyrics.[13] In perspectivist exercises like "Thirteen Ways of Looking at a Blackbird" or "Sea Surface Full of Clouds," the thing itself – whether a jar, a landscape, or a flock of pigeons – constellates senses of order for the perceiver. Each poem illustrates the poet discovering, as does the avuncular figure in "Le Monocle de Mon Oncle," "That fluttering things have so distinct a shade."(CP 18). It was perhaps inevitable that this discovery should incur the consequences of its own relativism. No longer could Stevens continue to illustrate the "maker's rage to order words of the sea" out of a barren reality. He had to "be / In the difficulty of what it is to be" (CP 381).

   It may seem superfluous to point out that this destructive poetics of Stevens' later style increasingly manifests itself in long poems. Their length is no small factor in their method, providing the imagination with a capacious field for exercising its faculties. We tend to think of the Modernist long poem in terms of its formal strategies of collage and pastiche, its generic preference for epic or dramatic modes, its thematic concerns with historical and cultural renewal. Stevens offers a distinct alternative to this paradigm by offering a version of the Romantic crisis poem in which the modulations of the poet's attentions become the poem's subject and ultimate verification. Unlike their Romantic precursors ("Dejection, An Ode," "Alastor," "Tintern Abbey"), Stevens' long poems do not appeal to some ultimate value (Joy, Truth, Beauty) to resolve the contrarieties introduced, even though they may utilize such abstractions as polemical centers for meditation. This form of long, exploratory poem has become one of the primary models for contemporary poets in their attempt to move beyond the single, self-sufficient lyric to the "poem of a life." Works such as A. R. Ammons' *Sphere*, Robert Duncan's *Passages*, Robert Kelly's *The Loom*, John Berryman's *Dream Songs*, John Ashbery's *Three Poems*, and James Merrill's *The Changing Light at Sandover* could be seen as variations on this mode.

Hermeneutic criticism has seized upon such poems as central to its discussion of a distinctly Postmodern poetics. Using Heidegger's analysis of Dasein in *Being and Time*, this criticism sees the open-ended, processual style of Stevens' long poems as destructive, both in literary and philosophical terms. As a text, "Notes toward a Supreme Fiction" (so the reading might go) proposes no strategies of closure, no consistent pattern of rhetorical figures, no mythological centers of sustaining narratives. In fact, as the opening cantos indicate, the very lack of such formal cultural signs inaugurates the poem: "Phoebus is dead, ephebe. But Phoebus was / A name for something that never could be named." The poet is thus able to step beyond the closed, spatial text of high Modernism into a more speculative, temporarily generative text whose end is not literary history but existential disclosure. As a philosophical project, the authentically Postmodern poem dis-covers *(aletheia)* or uncovers the temporal nature of Being, not by reference to some cultural cyclicity on the order of Yeats or Pound, but through its momentary, wandering interrogation. This "endlessly elaborating poem," as Stevens calls it, is able to work out the fullest implications of its subject by constantly exposing itself to change.[14]

I have presented this brief overview of the hermeneutic position because it has become, for better or worse, one of the major forums for examining the Postmodern long poem. I have discussed the advantages and limitations of this reading elsewhere.[15] I would like to suggest here that while such interpretation says much about the temporality of texts, it suggests even more about the temporality of their reception – the way in which the reader, lacking any stable interpretive counters, must engage directly the poet's explorations. Stevens was acutely conscious of this dimension, in theory and in practice:

> Anyone who has read a long poem day after day, as for example
> *The Faerie Queene*, knows how the poem comes to possess the

reader and how it naturalizes him in its own imagination and liberates him there. (NA 50)

The complexity of "Notes," its syntactic and linguistic play, its endless rearrangement of point of view, are all part of this naturalization process by which the poem "refreshes life so that we share, / For a moment, the first idea" (NA 382).

"Notes" is no *Faerie Queene,* however potent its personifications and fables. As its title implies, the poem does not propose completion or closure. It is tentative, accumulative, speculative. The preposition in its title stresses the series' projective stance. Where in an earlier period Stevens might have made notes "on" the theme of a supreme fiction, this poem may only point "toward." Both subject and method are concisely embodied in the opening lines of Canto VII of the opening section:

It feels good as it is without the giant,
A thinker of the first idea. Perhaps
The truth depends on a walk around a lake,

A composing as the body tires, a stop
To see hepatica, a stop to watch
A definition growing certain and

A wait within that certainty   (CP 386)

This passage described what Heidegger might call the "forestructure" *(Vorhabe)* of Stevens' metaphysics. The truth may no longer be grounded in a first cause, a "thinker of the first idea." In the desultory way of the poem itself, the truth "depends on a walk around a lake." Stevens resists analogy; the truth is not "like" a walk but depends upon the natural circumstance – the weather, water, hepatica to be viewed – as well as upon those acts of pausing, observing, and meandering by which the natural is absorbed. The definition of a supreme fiction never becomes certain; it grows toward certainty.

The occasion for this passage is similar to that in John Ashbery's "The Skaters." There the image of skaters gliding in random trajectories over a frozen surface serves as a model for the composing process as well as for cognitive acts. Ashbery does not represent skaters in his poem; rather, he "skates" himself, pausing to "watch / A definition growing certain" in random observations:

A great wind lifted these cardboard panels
Horizontal in the air. At once the perspective with the horse
Disappeared in a bigarrure of squiggly lines. The image with
    the crocodile in it became no longer apparent.

Thus a great wind cleanses, as a new ruler
Edits new laws, sweeping the very breath of the streets
Into posterior trash.[16]

Ashbery's use of definite article and demonstrative pronoun presumes an intimacy with the reader, even though the scene being described has no contextual referent. We are asked to witness the poet's witness, not to verify the accuracy of his perceptions against the proof of the world. Like Stevens, Ashbery is "not ready / To line phrases with the costly stuff of explanation," because this can only supplement a paraphrase for that which exists as sheer potential. Both poets realize that in the long poem, as Ashbery puts it,

> the carnivorous
> Way of these lines is to devour their own nature, leaving
> Nothing but a bitter impression of absence, which as we know
>   involves presence, but still.
> Nevertheless these are fundamental absences, struggling to
>   get up and be off themselves.[17]

As Ashbery's oxymoron indicates, the absences created by poetry are "fundamental," as basic to creation as the ice upon which the skaters skate and yet as ephemeral as the pattern of the skaters' tracks. To create an "absence in reality" is not to add to or subtract from the world but to circulate within it, as Stevens says, "Until merely going round is a final good" (CP 405).

Ashbery's casual, discursive tone is essential to the process, a way of negotiating between poles of presence and absence without assuming a fixed perspective. What may appear as a dandyish mode of diffidence actually represents a more complex response to the difficulties of positing a self-sufficient subject that orders the perceived world by means of some comprehensive rhetoric. Neither of the Modernist poles – Imagist directness nor New Critical irony and impersonality – offers a sufficient alternative to the crisis of self-presence that has emerged in the recent period. One offers an ideal of limitation, the other of mediation; both imply a degree of authorial control and detachment whose boundaries contemporary poets are eager to efface. And while Stevens' tone is not that of Ashbery, he offers an analogously problematic perspective in which no one voice in the poem is constitutive, in which the speaking subject becomes one of the many fictions on the way to what he calls the "monster Myself."

Stevens' bounty to Ashbery and other ephebes would seem to be "intricate evasions of as." His favorite position, as a philosophical poet, is to be moving between the poles of oppositions, attempting to "compound the imagination's Latin with / The lingua franca et jocundissima" (CP 397). Commentators have amply considered his debts in this relativism to Nietzsche, Bergson, Whitehead, James, Husserl, and others. It seems pointless to argue against Stevens as a philosophical poet, as does Helen Vendler, in favor of some inner narrative among the poems. More pertinent for our concern with contemporary poetics is the way in which those ideas are made manifest in particular formal strategies.

As a philosophical poet Stevens is not a particularly profound thinker; he tends throughout his work to reframe a rather elementary conflict between the imagination and reality. But few poets have ever embodied – "blooded" – abstractions in sensuous language more effectively than Stevens. (His titles alone would seem to have generated a subgenre of philosophical epigram among recent poets.) In the early poetry, this sensuous rendering of ideas manifests itself in the brilliant colorations of "Sunday Morning" or "Sea Surface Full of Clouds," in which "pungent oranges and bright, green wings" or "chop-house chocolate / And sham umbrellas" provide an almost expressionist surface for the poet's interrogations. His images are seldom tied to single objects or landscapes but tend to fracture, exfoliate, reform like the clouds that endlessly populate his poems. There is no easy tenor–vehicle relationship to his metaphors; they refer less to things or concepts than to themselves as material objects. As J. Hillis Miller observes, "[they] entirely contain their own reality"[18] to the extent that a blackbird, a pineapple, or a sea surface must be perpetually "put together" in order to "be" at all.

What is more pertinent to our concern with the later poems is Stevens' treatment of language as a system – its acoustics, its syntax, its pragmatics – in dramatizing ideas. When, at the end of "The Snow Man," Stevens invokes the "Nothing that is not there and the nothing that is" (CP 10), he provides a linguistic equivalent to a paradox for which images are entirely inadequate. His double negatives literally produce a "nothing" that is both full and empty at the same time. When he titles a poem, "Le Monocle de Mon Oncle," as Geoffrey Hartman points out, he captures in the minute phonemic difference between two words something of the larger semantic resonance of the poem – the ironic portrayal of the uncle, metonymically figured in his eyepiece.[19] This kind of operative or performative use of language has had an increasingly important function for contemporary poets as a way of writing a poetry of ideas within the very terms that those ideas present.[20] Two examples from "Notes" and one from a contemporary poet will serve as illustration.

In the famous fourth section of "It Must be Abstract," Stevens mocks mimesis by providing a series of modifiers that refuse to modify:

We are the mimics. Clouds are pedagogues
The air is not a mirror but bare board,
Coulisse bright-dark, tragic chiaroscuro

And comic color of the rose, in which
Abysmal instruments make sounds like pips
Of the sweeping meanings that we add to them.   (CP 384)

The general theme of this section is the impossibility of arriving at a truly objective perception of reality: "Adam in Eden was the father of Descartes / And Eve made air the mirror of herself." But air is not a mirror; it is an emptiness that we must fill, even though we are taught by clouds ("pedagogues") how solid that air can be. To dramatize the fact that in order to learn, we must already have projected human qualities and meanings onto nature, Stevens creates a series of phrases that are quite literally "fictions of air." The theatrical implications of "bare board" lead to "Coulisse bright-dark," which is then supplemented by "tragic chiaroscuro" and "comic color of the rose," each modifier giving a slightly different substance to air, dramatizing it by oxymoron. In two lines we have both tragedy and comedy, air and substance, stage and reality, light and dark, barrenness and flower, monochrome and color. Stevens' point in this elegant subordination is that we live in a "Theater / Of Trope," a world that must be framed as fiction in order to know it as fact. Stevens' phrases occupy the appropriate syntactical positions to modify "air," but instead of giving it form they only provide shadings and contrasts, abstract color and nuance. By means of this chiaroscuro Stevens is able to use language to mirror without relying on an object to be reflected, thus extending and elaborating his postlapsarian theme.

My second example of Stevens' performative use of language could be viewed as an outgrowth of the first. In Canto III of "It Must Give Pleasure" he again addressed repetition and mimicry, this time with regard to the problem of incarnation:

A lasting visage in a lasting bush,
A face of stone in an unending red,
Red-emerald, red-slitted-blue, a face of slate,

An ancient forehead hung with heavy hair,
The channel slots of rain, the red-rose-red
And weathered and the ruby-water-worn,

The vines around the throat, the shapeless lips,
The frown like serpents basking on the brow,
The spent feeling leaving nothing of itself,

Red-in-red repetitions never going
Away, a little rusty, a little rouged,
A little roughened and ruder, a crown

The eye could not escape, a red renown
Blowing itself upon the tedious ear.
An effulgence faded, dull cornelian

Too venerably used. That might have been.
It might and might have been. But as it was,
A dead shepherd brought tremendous chords from hell

And bade the sheep carouse. Or so they said.
Children in love with them brought early flowers
And scattered them about, no two alike.   (CP 400)

Stevens' comments on this poem indicate that, at one level, the problem is less the nature of deity, that "lasting visage in a lasting bush," than the conditions of its worship:

> The first thing one sees of any deity is the face, so that the elementary idea of God is a face: a lasting visage in a lasting bush. Adoration is a form of face to face. When the compulsion to adoration grows less, or merely changes, unless the change is complete, the face changes and, in the case of a face at which one has looked for a long time, changes that are slight may appear to the observer to be melodramatic. We struggle with the face, see it everywhere & try to express the changes. (L 438)

This last sentence could serve as a description of Stevens' method in the canto itself: a struggle to see the face of an incomprehensible idea in its changeability and to "express the changes" in our perception of it. In order to focus his own perception, he describes a colossus, a "face of stone" reminiscent of Ozymandias, not standing mute and abandoned. This statue is a variation on others in Stevens' writing, from the equestrian statues in "The Noble Rider and the Sound of Words" to that of General Du Pay in "Notes." As with these others, the ideals which the statue represents have lost their relationship to the reality from which they sprang. The face no longer inspires; it is "An effulgence faded."

Stevens' secular task is to resurrect from this shell of deity the possibility of change. He does so thematically by introducing the image of a "dead shepherd" who combines both Christ and Orpheus, Word and speaker of the Word. Helen Vendler worries that this image, so briefly introduced, is "a much less successful invention than the colossal head."[21] This might be so, were it not for the qualifying phrase, "Or so they said," that so severely brackets the authority of this apotheosis, drawing attention to the essentially fictional nature of the new Logos. Stevens provides his own transformative act, linguistically, by decreasing the "face of stone" by a series of variations on the word "red." He first describes the head in minute detail, cataloging its "ancient forehead," its "shapeless lips," but quickly turns from description to evocation. The "unending red" background in which the head exists – the red of barren reality – soon becomes "Red-emerald, red-slitted blue." Finally, Stevens rings changes on the word itself, providing "Red-in-red repetitions" in the subtle modulations of "rusty," "roughed," "roughened," "ruder," "red renown," "cornelian." Stevens is able both to sustain the endurance of reality (an unending red) in the creation of supreme fictions and, at the same time, to suggest the variability of that fiction as the perspectives from which it is viewed change. Within his Nietzschean allegory, Stevens is able to release the Logos as origin, source, first idea to its function as language, play, Orphic transformation. Like the words themselves, variations on a single term, the flowers brought by "Children in love with them" are "no two alike."

My third example, from a contemporary poet, Michael Palmer, deals with certain fallacies in what Palmer calls in his title, "The Project of Linear Inquiry." His concern is to present a series of postulates that seem to fall into a logical sequence but which are diverted by other associations. The poem opens as follows:

> [Let a be taken as . . .]
> a liquid line beneath the skin
> and b where the blue tiles meet
> body and the body's bridge
> a seeming road here, endless
>
> rain pearling light
> chamber after chamber
> of dust-weighted air
> the project of seeing things
> so to speak, or things seen
>
> namely a hand, namely
> the logic of the hand
> holding a bell or clouded lens
> the vase perched impossibly near the edge
> obscuring the metal tines.[22]

We are first introduced to an incomplete postulate in brackets – "Let a be taken as . . ." – that, although fragmentary, is nonetheless partially continued in the next line by means of the indefinite article: "a liquid line beneath the skin." We then encounter a second postulate, this time without brackets: "and *b* where the blue tiles meet." Instead of terminating, however, this phrase continues into other words beginning with "b" ("body" and "body's bridge"). This progress from a to b, from liquid line to the meeting point of blue tiles (another kind of line), then leads to other linear forms, a "bridge" and a "road." Contextual frames established in one line are dismantled in the next; and semantic elements from one line create new referential frames in subsequent lines. Whatever proof had been intended by the sequence of postulation has been overtaken by a series of imagistic and linguistic substitutions that, in a sense, obey one kind of logic by means of another. Lines nine and ten, the most Stevensian lines of the example, could serve as a definition of Palmer's problem, "the project of seeing things / so to speak," which I would paraphrase as the problem of reconciling phenomena, received experientially or sensually, with a logical grammar. Each image is given precise definition ("the vase perched impossibly near the edge / obscuring the metal tines"), yet images do not combine to complete a single picture. Instead, signification occurs, despite the failure of "linear inquiry" to account for all aspects of the production of meaning. Palmer shows us not the *results* of inquiry but the *processes,* not the proof but the project.

Part of the difficulty in reading both this and the Stevens examples is that their words function more as instances than as signs. We must learn to read diacritically as well as semantically. When Stevens says of the poem, "It must be abstract," he means abstraction not as generalization but, paradoxically, as the intensification of particularity to the point where a word no longer exists within any conventional context. In order to see a thing we must "unsee" it, abstract it and defamiliarize it, create a language with the same freshness and poignancy as the thing itself. And unlike the Symbolist attempt to create, through unexpected conjunction and association, a world quite apart from the one we inhabit, Stevens invites closer and closer participation with a world we have forgotten how to see.

What I have described as Stevens' linguistic abstraction accompanies a central romantic theme of personal and spiritual alienation. The fall of man, so the familiar version goes, is a fall into a demythologized world, a world of neutral signs, in which an Adamic language of unmediated presence has been lost. To paraphrase one of Stevens' titles, man lives in a "description without a place." "Notes toward a Supreme Fiction" takes as one of its premises that man is estranged from what is most familiar:

> From this the poem springs: that we live in a place
> That is not our own and, much more, not ourselves   (CP 383)

This alienation is both destructive and creative: In order to conceive of a place as "ours," we must destroy it as "other" and naturalize it in our own terms. This act of transformation generates another kind of reality, "the supreme fictions without which we are unable to conceive of [the world]." The sense of alienation that Stevens feels is a prerequisite to any metaphysics whatever and serves as an important corrective to the idealizing tendencies to which he was always subject. My earlier reference to Heraclitus (man's estrangement from what is familiar) should also be read as a reference to the many contemporary poets who have used this fragment to describe the same sense of disparity between place and imagination, thing and word, precept and concept.

At first glance, contemporary poetry might seem to reflect quite the opposite sense of place. Gary Snyder's identification with the Pacific Northwest; Charles Olson's dedication to Gloucester; Robert Bly's association with the northern Midwest; and Frank O'Hara's passion for New York would suggest a regionalist ethos entirely inhospitable to Stevens' propositional landscapes. We are used to thinking of contemporary poets' strong identification with locale in terms of their desire to establish contact with atavistic, aboriginal forces latent in specific places. We are told that, reacting against the Modernist fetish of European high culture, contemporary poets have taken up Whitman's and Emerson's call for an American epic based on American soil and have approved Williams' struggle to maintain "contact" with local, indigenous subjects. But this "immanentist" position, as Charles Altieri characterizes it,[23] with its precedents in Wordsworthian pantheism and Emersonian idealism, is the second part of a two-stage process. Preceding it is the recognition of essential solitude and a sense of disparity between the world of intransigent glyphs and one's own language. A few quotations will illustrate the variety of ways in which this rift is expressed:

> we want to go home and exist in a quietude like merriment
> but we can't go home as ourselves but wearing the faces
> of many answering things until, faceless, we can't tell we're
> home because we are.   (A. R. Ammons)

Words are what sticks to the real. We use them to push the real, to drag the real into the poem. They are what we hold on with, nothing else. They are as valuable in themselves as rope with nothing to be tied to.   (Jack Spicer)

I am certain, without ever having been there, I would be bored to sickness walking through Gloucester. Buildings as such are not important. The wash of the sea is not interesting in itself, that is luxuria, a degrading thing, people as they stand, must be created.   (Edward Dorn)

What [Poe] wanted was connected with no particular place;
therefore it *must* be where he *was*.   (William Carlos Williams)

and I have lost what is always and everywhere
present, the scene of my selves, the occasion of these ruses,
which I myself and singly must now kill
and save the serpent in their midst.[24]   (Frank O'Hara)

Each quotation could be read as a variation on the Stevens lines quoted
earlier. Place offers no solace by itself; the wash of the sea, the buildings
of the town, are entirely separate from the poem. Words, by themselves,
are similarly inadequate; as Spicer says, they are "what sticks to the real
. . . as valuable in themselves as rope with nothing to be tied to." Ammons'
"home" and O'Hara's "scene" may be attained only by effacing the ideal
of a central self "until, faceless, we can't tell we're / / home because we
are." The disparity felt is not the existential agony of a Sartre or a Kafka;
it is rather the necessary occasion by which the familiar may be recognized as such. In numerous contemporary poems, from Adrienne Rich's
"Diving into the Wreck," to Sylvia Plath's "The Colossus," to Charles
Olson's "The Librarian," the poet encounters an alien landscape whose
outlines are familiar but whose terms of order and coherence remain
obscure. The poet uses the poem to investigate this area, whether based
on fragments from a dream, a series of field notes, a day's random occasions, or lines from a poem. The transition from this "not-at-homeness"
to "home" is described vividly by Robert Duncan:

> Often I am Permitted to Return to a Meadow
>
> as if it were a scene made-up by the mind,
> that is not mine, but is a made place,
>
> that is mine, it is so near to the heart[25]

Duncan describes a place that could be the poem itself – "mine" because
"near to the heart," yet "not mine" because received from without. Access
to this meadow is gained by "permission," not by demand. The poet
experiences the same uncanny visitation as the dreamer who receives the
dream both as a foreign text and as a story in which he is the central
character.

The allegory of man's alienation from reality and his subsequent marriage *to* reality is present in all of Stevens' poems, from Crispin attempting to "stem verboseness in the sea" to the Interior Paramour, who makes
a "dwelling in the evening air." In "Notes toward a Supreme Fiction,"
it takes the form of a "mystic marriage in Catawba" between a "great
captain and the maiden Bawda." The bride, as her name implies, is part
of the place itself and not about it:

They married well because the marriage place
Was what they loved. It was neither heaven nor hell.
They were love's characters come face to face.   (CP 401)

The place in which (to which) they are married is not a symbolic place,
guaranteed by biblical decree, but a place made of themselves in the same
way that Williams feels Poe created his poetry. Stevens' Catawba, like
his New Haven, Key West, or Tennessee, is a wilderness from which
springs desire:

And not to have is the beginning of desire.
To have what is not is its ancient cycle.
It is desire at the end of winter, when

It observes the effortless weather turning blue
And sees the myosotis on its bush
Being virile, it hears the calendar hymn.

It knows that what it has is what is not
And throws it away like a thing of another time,
As morning throws off stale moonlight and shabby sleep.
                                                    (CP 382)

Out of this dialectic of desire comes the openness to change that
Stevens feels is necessary to the poem, a condition that Robert Duncan
calls "permission" to enter the field of creative life. Thus a "place of first
permission" exists not as part of some archetypal ahistorical principle but
as that which projects a possible future, "As morning throws off stale
moonlight and shabby sleep." Place is the becoming conscious of more
than place, transforming spatial reality into occasion. As Charles Olson
says of geography,

It is the imposing
of all those antecedent predecessions, the precessions

of me, the generation of those facts
which are my words, it is coming

from all that I no longer am, yet am,
the slow westward motion of

more than I am[26]

In this essay I have resisted the term "Postmodernism" almost successfully – "resisted" because the term now serves too many masters,
and "almost" because, like any fiction, supreme or critical, it must be

continually reinvented. As a literary historical term, Postmodernism serves the relatively simple purpose of differentiating between one generation and another. As a critical term, it implies a constellation of responses to the Kantian aesthetic revolution as formulated by the Symbolist poetics of the New Critics. Stevens, along with Gertrude Stein, Beckett, and Williams, occupies a central position in the transition between Modernism and Postmodernism. He inherits an ideal of pure poetry – even a theory of correspondences – from Symbolism, but the direction of his linguistic experimentation is toward something quite different from Mallarmé's mystical nether realm or Baudelaire's forest of symbols. And although he states that "Poetry / Exceeding music must take the place / Of empty heaven and its hymns" (CP 167), his is no Paterian religion of art. Stevens' linguistic indeterminacy is directed toward a determinate world, a fact that links him more to Williams than to his other contemporaries. But where Williams focuses on the thing, Stevens focuses on the apprehension of the thing. Both believe in the essential worth of red wheelbarrows and jars, but they find themselves looking at these objects from entirely different perspectives. As a Modernist, Stevens occupies a position somewhere between Henry James and Charles Ives – between an artist who made the house of fiction out of fluctuating moods and subtle inflections, and an artist for whom the criteria of performability and realization seemed an unnecessary bother. Finally, Stevens' is a critical poetry, as I believe contemporary poetry, in its best estate, can be: critical of its own ability to achieve a supreme fiction at the expense of the world, critical of language in service to a transcendental ideal.

But Stevens' critical function stops here, at the border of institutions and ideologies. His well-known difficulties in responding to the specific conditions of historical change reflect a willingness to uphold the barrier between aesthetic and material production. If "Life consists / Of propositions about life," as he says in "Men Made Out of Words," there is the danger that all such propositions are equally valuable and that their origin is entirely monologic rather than part of human dialogue. It has been for later poets to take up the kind of propositional, philosophical poetry that Stevens began and direct it toward particular social and ideological forms. Works like Ed Dorn's *Slinger,* David Antin's talk pieces, and the work of the language poets seem to extend Stevens' propositional logic into investigations of discursive and pragmatic communicational models. "Notes toward a Supreme Fiction" may now have become "Notes toward the Ideologies of Supreme Fictions."

I do not mean to imply that the single achievement of Postmodernist poetry, with or without Stevens, has been its politicization of poetry, but rather that in undermining certain formalist models of high Modernism, it has attempted to enlarge the dialogic and discursive possibilities of poetry. It has called into question the nature of the single, self-sufficient subject, while opening a dialogue with the reader as coproducer of the text. It has brought the material nature of its own creation into sharp focus, treating poetic language not as a separate, sacrosanct domain (the poetic function) but as a dimension of sign and thus a social product. If Wallace Stevens seems an unlikely benefactor of these events, it is because he so successfully provided us with the means to interrogate and refashion his pedagogy in our own terms. "We reason of these things with later reason," the poet reasons, "And we make of what we see, what we see clearly / And have seen, a place dependent on ourselves." We might add: a place dependent on ourselves in Wallace Stevens.

NOTES

1   Robert Creeley, "Letter to Charles Olson, April 28, 1950," in *Charles Olson and Robert Creeley: The Complete Correspondence,* vol. 1, ed. George F. Butterick (Santa Barbara, Calif.: Black Sparrow Press, 1980), p. 22.

2   Robert Creeley, "Letter to Charles Olson, June 5, 1950," in *Charles Olson and Robert Creeley: The Complete Correspondence,* vol. 1, p. 79.

3   S. T. Coleridge, *Biographia Literaria,* ed. James Engell and W. Jackson Bate (Princeton: Princeton University Press, 1983), II, 12.

4   See Donald Wesling's extensive discussion of this phrase in his "The Prosodies of Free Verse," *Harvard Studies in English,* vol. 2 (Cambridge: Harvard University Press, 1971) and *The Chances of Rhyme: Device and Modernity* (Berkeley: University of California Press, 1980), chapter 1.

5   "Adagia," in Wallace Stevens, *Opus Posthumous* (New York: Knopf, 1957), p. 164, hereinafter abbreviated as OP. Subsequent references to Wallace Stevens' works will be abbreviated in the text as follows: *The Collected Poems of Wallace Stevens* (New York: Knopf, 1954), CP; *Letters of Wallace Stevens,* ed. Holly Stevens (New York: Knopf, 1966), L; *The Necessary Angel* (New York: Knopf, 1951), NA.

6   *The Wallace Stevens Journal* 3 (Fall, 1979).

7   Harold Bloom, *A Map of Misreading* (New York: Oxford University Press, 1975), p. 3.

8   See in addition to *A Map of Misreading* Bloom's *The Anxiety of Influence: A Theory of Poetry* (New York: Oxford University Press, 1975) and *The Ringers in the Tower: Studies in Romantic Tradition* (Chicago: University of Chicago Press, 1971).

9   "An Interview with John Ashbery," *San Francisco Review of Books* 3 (November 1977), 9.

10   I have discussed the limitations of Bloom's "revisionary ratios" in "Ekphrasis and the Postmodern Painter Poem," *Journal of Aesthetics and Art Criticism* 42 (Fall 1983), 69–79.

11 For critiques of Bloom's theory of influence from two widely differing perspectives, see Paul A. Bove, *Destruction Poetics: Heidegger and Modern American Poetry* (New York: Columbia University Press, 1980), pp. 7–31; and Frank Lentricchia, *After the New Criticism* (Chicago: University of Chicago Press, 1980), pp. 318–46.

12 Louis Zukofsky, "For Wallace Stevens," in *Prepositions: The Collected Critical Essays of Louis Zukofsky* (Berkeley: University of California Press, 1981), pp. 26–27.

13 Roy Harvey Pearce, "Wallace Stevens: The Life of the Imagination," in *Wallace Stevens: A Collection of Critical Essays*, ed. Marie Borroff (Englewood Cliffs, N.J.: Prentice-Hall, 1963), pp. 111–32.

14 On hermeneutic approaches to Postmodernism, see Bove, *Destructive Poetics;* William V. Spanos, "Breaking the Circle: Hermeneutics as Dis-closure," *Boundary 2*, vol. 2 (Winter 1977), 421–57; Spanos, "Heidegger, Kierkegaard, and the Hermeneutic Circle: Towards a Postmodern Theory of Interpretation as Dis-closure," *Boundary 2*, vol. 4 (Winter 1976), 455–88; Joseph N. Riddel, "A Somewhat Polemical Introduction: The Elliptical Poem," *Genre* 11 (Winter 1978), 459–77; Riddel, "Interpreting Stevens: An Essay on Poetry and Thinking," *Boundary 2*, vol. 1 (Fall 1972), 49–97.

15 See Davidson, "Ekphrasis and the Postmodern Painter Poem" (note 10) and Davidson, "Archeologist of Morning: Charles Olson, Edward Dorn and Historical Method," *ELH* 47 (1980), 158–79.

16 John Ashbery, "The Skaters," in *Rivers and Mountains* (New York: Holt, 1970), pp. 36–37.

17 Ashbery, "The Skaters," p. 39.

18 J. Hillis Miller, "Wallace Stevens," in *Poets of Reality: Six Twentieth-Century Writers* (New York: Atheneum, 1969), p. 228.

19 Geoffrey H. Hartman, "The Voice of the Shuttle: Language from the Point of View of Literature," in *Beyond Formalism: Literary Essays 1958–1970* (New Haven: Yale University Press, 1970), p. 341.

20 My use of the term "performative" is an adaption of J. L. Austin's term, described in *How to Do Things with Words* (Cambridge, Mass.: Harvard University Press, 1975), although I realize that Austin is speaking within the context of pragmatics and I am describing a phenomenon in rhetoric. Still, the spirit, if not the letter, of Austin's approach is to describe utterances that *do* rather than represent something, even if the sphere in which they perform is primarily that of social discourse.

21 Helen Vendler, *On Extended Wings: Wallace Stevens' Longer Poems* (Cambridge, Mass.: Harvard University Press, 1971), p. 175.

22 Michael Palmer, *Notes for Echo Lake* (San Francisco: North Point Press, 1981), p. 58.

23 Charles Altieri, "From Symbolist Thought to Immanence: The Ground of Postmodern American Poetics," *Boundary 2*, vol. 1 (Spring 1973), 605–41.

24 A. R. Ammons, *Sphere: The Form of a Motion* (New York: Norton, 1974), p. 22; Jack Spicer, "After Lorca," in *The Collected Books of Jack Spicer* (Santa Barbara, Calif.: Black Sparrow Press, 1975), p. 25; Edward Dorn, "What I

See in *The Maximus Poems,*" in *The Poetics of the New American Poetry,* ed. Donald Allen and Warren Tallman (New York: Grove Press, 1973), pp. 298–99; William Carlos Williams, *In the American Grain* (New York: New Directions, 1956), p. 220; Frank O'Hara, "In Memory of My Feelings," in *The Selected Poems of Frank O'Hara,* ed. Donald Allen (New York: Random House, 1974), p. 110.

25   Robert Duncan, "Often I Am Permitted to Return to a Meadow," in *The Opening of the Field* (New York: Grove Press, 1960), p. 7.

26   Charles Olson, "Maximus to Gloucester, Letter 27 (withheld)" in *Maximus Poems IV, V, VI* (London: Cape Goliard Press, 1968), n.p.

Index